The Entrepreneur's Guide to Managing Growth and Handling Crises

The Entrepreneur's Guide

CJ Rhoads, Series Editor

The Entrepreneur's Guide to Managing Growth and Handling Crises

Theo J. van Dijk

Westport, Connecticut
London

Library of Congress Cataloging-in-Publication Data

Dijk, Theo J. van.
  The entrepreneur's guide to managing growth and handling crises / Theo J. van Dijk.
      p. cm. — (The entrepreneur's guide, ISSN 1939–2478)
  Includes bibliographical references and index.
  ISBN-13: 978–0–275–99603–1 (alk. paper)
  1. New business enterprises—Management. 2. Small business—Growth. 3. Entrepreneurship. I. Title.
  HD62.5.D55 2008
  658.4'06—dc22   2007039908

British Library Cataloguing in Publication Data is available.

Library of Congress Catalog Card Number: 2007039908
ISBN-13: 978–0–275–99603–1
ISSN: 1939–2478

First published in 2008

Praeger Publishers, 88 Post Road West, Westport, CT 06881
An imprint of Greenwood Publishing Group, Inc.
www.praeger.com

Printed in the United States of America

∞

The paper used in this book complies with the Permanent Paper Standard issued by the National Information Standards Organization (Z39.48–1984).

10 9 8 7 6 5 4 3 2 1

We have met the enemy and he is us.
Walt Kelly

Contents

Acknowledgments

The many nameless but pretty essential and effective contributors to this, my first book, are without a doubt the entrepreneurs and their employees in the many industries and countries that I have been associated with. To them and to the ones I am currently still (in 2007) engaged with goes my supreme gratitude for being such a target-rich environment.

To my exceptionally gifted professional friends David and Ken Wright of Wright Consultancy, Dublin, Ireland, my great appreciation for recognizing that what I had been doing for the last twenty years or so was well worth writing about and, what is more, for reading the very first unedited version of the manuscript and nonetheless encouraging me to keep at it and with it. They were always available to share their penetrating views and sound ideas.

Another skilled professional friend and supporter, Vivian Byrne, Managing Director of CSA Ltd., Dublin, Ireland, also read the first unedited manuscript and helped me during many a one-to-one session with his unwavering enthusiasm and his razor-sharp insights.

Rien Smit, a once-upon-a-time colleague who did eventually find his niche as the Managing Director of Woningborg Advies b.v., the Netherlands, spent many years, much like me, helping SENIC businesses through their first major organizational crises. We often compared notes, swapped experiences, and sought each other's long-distance remote support when the goings got really tough.

Rick Oates, Jr., Partner & Talent Scouting Specialist of Construction Group International, Tonawanda, New York, has helped me more than he will ever realize in finding the faith to trust that really important decisions are best left to our Lord and that we should concentrate instead on getting ourselves all snarled up with the little insignificant ones. His support and his zest for life were an inspiration to me during many a period of turmoil.

Stan Kopaskie, former Vice President of Birdair, Inc., Amherst, New York, who always impressed me with his calm, collected, take-me-as-I-am dressed-down manner, gave me much down-to-earth advice, taught me not to take myself so seriously, and, above all, imparted this wisdom: When the chips are down you follow your instinct.

Ian Stewart, Director of Genesys Systems Ltd., Dublin, Ireland, was an eager reader and critic of the second version and has incorporated some of the SENIC antidotes into Genesys's approach to system implementations for growing entrepreneurial businesses.

Michel Meyerink, Managing Director of Mediaxplosion b.v. and Websitesdirect b.v., and Eric Noordermeer, Managing Partner of Albion Network Technologies b.v, two Dutch entrepreneurs, read the first manuscript and gave me blunt feedback. It took me awhile to get over that, but thanks anyway guys!

My two smart and beautiful daughters, Judith and Nicole, both read the first version of the manuscript and gave me their frank judgments. Their subtle female tact in nudging me gently but firmly to reconsider some pretty "I told you so" statements was quite phenomenal. They are so much more intelligent than I am.

My sincere appreciation goes out to Jeff Olson of Praeger. Jeff looked at the first version of the manuscript, decided to take on the project, and gently but firmly led me to the second, much improved, version. Then, applying one of his own slogans—"when there is no path, make one"—he actively promoted the project and hit pay dirt. He made me review the whole project once again so it could be part of Praeger's Entrepreneurs Guide Series. I agreed reluctantly—don't forget I already had invested the better part of a year in this, my first writing project—but then with renewed enthusiasm and his continued encouragement rewrote, cut and pasted, and added more material until he was satisfied. Looking back, the first two versions were really rough and nowhere near as comprehensive as the final one you presently hold in your hands. Many thanks, Jeff. You patiently and skillfully helped me fulfill one of my more important missions in life.

To my wonderful wife, Bridget, I owe undying gratitude—and not really because she read every word of every version that was produced over a period of well over a year while giving me her honest opinion—but primarily for her continued support and the sometimes required push to keep me focused. The untold story of the glories and defeats, the frustrations and successes, and the restless travels of a husband who always wanted to experience another entrepreneurial environment, another culture on another continent during another assignment are no doubt carved in her heart. Often the trials and tribulations of the work day came home to be vented in the private atmosphere of yet another rented dwelling. To her must go the ultimate credit of this book, for sticking with a husband, who after 38 years of marriage is still "a work in progress" and has so many dreams and missions that are yet to be conquered.

Eternal gratitude is reserved for my Heavenly Father, who determined that fateful evening on the May 2, 1993, in Riyadh, Saudi Arabia, that my mission on earth was not even close to completion and that I had to stick around a while longer until it was. Maybe this book is a tiny token of my gratitude to Him for giving me a second chance.

1

Impediments to Growth

The time has come for action—but what action?
General Franz Halder, Chief of the German General Staff (1938–1942)

You are to be congratulated! To reach the stage where your venture has survived the exciting start-up years is quite a feat. The company mortality rate for the early entrepreneurial phase is extremely high, especially during the first year. Few infant firms survive the first creative period of growth. Allow yourself a quick look back and be proud that you made it! It was tough but fun. You were in sole charge and in full control, making those vital instant key decisions and enjoying it! There were plenty of hurdles along the way but you overcame them all. Personal drive and perseverance—not to mention your trusted and dedicated team of employees—made it all possible. Your quest to grow the business and be even more successful and even more profitable appears to be well on track.

That's why your first crisis comes as quite a shock—not to mention the impact on your bank balance and already overstretched resources. What's more, this crisis always appears to happen at the very moment when you thought you were slipping and sliding smoothly into the senior leagues!

This book is about how a successful entrepreneur can better face the next major challenge. Greiner (1972)[1] called this follow-on period from the entrepreneurial phase "the first revolutionary crisis." This phrase often describes the transition period from *entrepreneur* to *owner-manager*, because the skills to be the "creator" and the skills to be the "leader or developer" are often mutually exclusive.

A lot has been written about entrepreneurs. We have all read one or more of the rags-to-riches stories. Similarly, at the other end of the spectrum, the literature on management in large and multinational companies is almost exhaustive. But the challenging and often lengthy periods between these two extremes are seldom the subject of consideration. In particular, little has been said or written about the first revolutionary crisis. Even less has been written about the phase that comes after that, SENIC Businesses. This, then, is the subject of this book: the transition of the entrepreneurial phase via the first revolutionary crisis to the next phase, called the direction or autonomy phase.

Products and markets play an important role during this transition. But the make-or-break factors during this often extremely turbulent period are the behavior and characteristics of the entrepreneur, sometimes even the entrepreneur's family, the employees, and (if already brought on board), a general manager. They all play a role in what I call the SENIC business: Still Evolving, Now In Crisis.

SENIC Business: Still Evolving, Now In Crisis

A SENIC business is one that has more or less survived the exciting but anxious start-up years. SENIC businesses are still owned almost exclusively by the entrepreneur(s). But knowingly or unknowingly to all participants and bystanders, the entrepreneurial years have come to an end and the first organizational crisis has taken root. It has to be dealt with. Survival is once again at stake!

When and how entrepreneurial businesses reach this turbulent SENIC phase on the timeline of their overall lifespan is not really very important, in my opinion. Some businesses get there fast; others might take many years or sometimes even a few generations. It all depends and depended on the drive and ambition of the current entrepreneur. Take, for example, the corner shop where past generations have scratched a reasonable living, but then the fourth generation becomes ambitious (lucky, some would say) and decides to buy another corner shop, and another one and so on. The start-up phase of the business in this example has long since passed. But the point is that in the life cycle of this particular business, the first revolutionary crisis will probably be reached during the fourth generation. When incremental growth in turnover and staffing reaches a specific but difficult-to-predetermine level, the crisis will strike unannounced.

Considerable and sometimes critical changes are now required to give the newly arrived SENIC business a better-than-even chance during the next evolutionary period. This realization alone is a difficult notion to swallow for any entrepreneur and existing team. As an entrepreneur, you are not the most humble and patient of individual and your personally picked team of employees soon grasps that what is required is not necessarily in their favor and often not to their liking.

This is not a book on middle management in multinationals or top management in large or multinational organizations. This is a book on the circumstances that often exist in SENIC businesses after the initial entrepreneurial phase has run its course. Thus it is a guide to entrepreneurs and their staffs to enlighten, inform, and prepare them for the next phase. The first organizational crisis will not evaporate by itself. Action of some type or other is required.

THE CONTRIBUTION OF SENIC BUSINESSES

Surviving the entrepreneurial stage is important to the national economy, yet is often not spoken about, recognized, or published. Yet SENIC businesses are responsible for over 50 percent of all employment and, depending on which country they are in, contribute between 50 to 75 percent of gross national product.[2] Therefore, it is somewhat surprising that not more attention is paid to SENIC companies in the business literature. Most of the publicity and attention, particularly of the popular press and the academic fraternity, seem to be focused on the very large, multinational companies. Since little is said and even less is written about businesses of the SENIC variety, even though the majority of employees in the Western world—probably in the whole world—work for this type of business, I like to think that what is described in my book is what it's really like out there. So even if you are not an entrepreneur but work for an entrepreneurial company, you might recognize some of the issues described in the following chapters.

The businesses that have survived the creative start-up period have gained a measure of respectability, a client base, and some of the characteristics of an established organization. The entrepreneur's family is starting to show an interest as well. There is something to be divided! As an old Irish saying goes, "Where there's a will there's a relative."

The SENIC business's senior management—let's not refer to it as a management *team* as yet—tends to be made up of extremely loyal and hard-working employees. They are honorary members of the family, but with no voting rights, of course.

These and other employees of our SENIC businesses are often still stuck in a time warp, say the early seventeenth century, being treated practically like captive slaves to the greater glory of the entrepreneur. They are probably not aware of it.

SENIC All the Way

My own association with SENIC businesses spans three continents over the last twenty-odd years. I was usually the first professionally educated manager, if you like, that entered the playing field in order to prepare the organization for the next growth phase, whatever that was supposed to be.

Over the last twenty-odd years, I've worked with many entrepreneurs experiencing many problems. Sometimes the company had gotten into a hole that had been merrily dug deeper and deeper until it defied all normal logic of market dynamics and rational decision making. Sometimes, the situation was so badly out of control that you wondered why there were still any customers left. Perhaps you've seen similar situations:

- The entrepreneur who worked day and night with his faithful band of brothers but, unfortunately, the original idea did not seem to carry the business anymore.

- The company that had developed contempt for customers: "Hey, they want it on time as well? What's the matter with these customers? Can't they see we are doing our best?"
- The over-generous entrepreneur whose most trusted and loyal employees were not really very capable as senior managers. They had fallen upstairs into the "Peter Principle" bucket.[3]
- The extremely suspicious entrepreneur who thought that budgeting was only meant for control so that you "could find out how the SOBs were spending your money."
- The entrepreneur who didn't realize that if you gave people responsibility, you also had to seriously consider giving them—I know it hurts—*authority*.
- The inconsistent head-in-the-clouds entrepreneur who believed that creating chaotic situations was not the same as living in a dynamic environment.
- The overworked and completely stressed-out entrepreneurs who feel that fire fighting with leaking buckets can be fun and extremely satisfying, but don't realize that it's not necessarily productive.
- The entrepreneur with an engineering background who believed that standardization in machinery, tools, and equipment was a supplier's plot rather than a method to make the business run more smoothly when it came to engineering and maintenance (see Time Out 1.1).
- The many entrepreneurs who believed their nieces and nephews, perhaps recently graduated from college, were well suited for a senior position in their organizations.
- The large number of entrepreneurs who believed that accountants and lawyers always give sound business advice, and who might not understand that these advisors were possibly in there for the money.
- The overly headstrong entrepreneur who took everyone to court who disagreed with him, and who didn't realize that accountants charge by the hour.
- The fully matured Scrooge-type entrepreneur who expounded that "You could never trust employees because all they did was spend your money while you were trying to make it."
- The somewhat "stuck in a rut" entrepreneur who confused "twenty years experience" with "one year experience twenty times over."[4]
- The impatient entrepreneur who believed (to be fair, not without grounds) that ISO 9002 is a system that you can buy off the shelf.
- The not-so-streetwise entrepreneurs who were probably well aware of the distinction between tax avoidance and tax evasion, but maybe not the behaviors required!

Changes Are Afoot

We can all relate to some of the entrepreneurial experiences described. Successful entrepreneurs have not achieved post-entrepreneurial conditions by sitting back and letting others tell them what to do. However, what the examples illustrate are the symptoms that are part of the SENIC condition.

It Couldn't Happen to You—or Could It?
TIME OUT 1.1
How to Enjoy Your Hobby and Blame Your Staff for the Cost

One of the better examples of this dictum was a medium-sized transport company where eight different models of trucks (some of which were, to be charitable, in need of TLC) were employed in a fleet of fifty-four. This company operated on a border between two countries where lots of businesses were used to exploiting the price differences to their advantage.

After some consideration, I broached the subject of standardization with the owner. He asked me to prepare a report to show him why this would make sense. After many a night of gathering data, preparing statistics and graphs, and seeking the help of a friend, a transport manager in a large logistics company, I sat down with the owner who appeared very impressed indeed. We agreed that we would standardize the fleet to no more than two types, but he would retain the decision on the types of truck. As he certainly knew a thing or two about trucks, I gladly left that decision to him.

I had not been on leave for a while and it was about Christmas time, so I left for a week's vacation. Coming back I noticed two well-used but to me foreign trucks in the yard. One of the mechanics told me that Mick, the owner, had been across the border with him and brought them back. Naturally they were of different pedigree than we had agreed on.

Mick was significant by his absence, because he normally ate, slept, and drank at the yard. When I eventually tracked him down, he behaved like a naughty boy with his hand caught in the cookie jar. However, after a while he could not take it any longer and angrily shouted at me, "They were a bargain. I could not resist it, it was my decision, and after all I never really agreed with your so-called plan."

Who can argue with such eloquent logic?

Treating the symptoms does not eliminate the root cause. If the cause of the problem is not addressed, it will reoccur and (in accordance with Murphy's Law) probably be even worse than before. Often the very essence of the working environment so cherished by the entrepreneur and his employees needs to be transformed. Thus, reading between the lines so far, you can no doubt pick out some of the most acute impediments to growth, namely:

- the lack of an effective organization
- no real delegation of authorities and responsibilities
- the lack of formal systems
- lack of a proper definition of customers

These issues may sound too simple to be the problem, and that is exactly why a lot of entrepreneurs are tripped up. Thus remember, the difficulty is not the identification of the problem. The challenge lies in the execution of the detail. You don't just wave a magic wand and introduce authority and responsibility to your staff. It's a long and arduous learning process. Also, the chances are that the employees of the first hour are often not suited for some of the management tasks ahead.

Then there is the really curious question, "Who exactly are our customers?" Nothing is more difficult for an entrepreneur than to say "no" to what appears to be a potential customer but, believe you me, you can't satisfy them all. In contrast, sometimes the original, successful product formula needs to be adjusted to appeal to a wider, well-defined customer base. One thing is for certain: your company needs to change and you, the entrepreneur, need to change with it.

Success Is Not Guaranteed

Some SENIC businesses will continue to be very successful despite the problems. Others survive but are badly bruised by the SENIC experience. Some do not survive at all. In hindsight it is always easy to deliberate why successes were booked and failures were experienced. After a success or failure, all the experts can tell you why certain things worked and others didn't.

That's not to say failure isn't useful. We learn as much from some of the failures as we do from the successes. But most entrepreneurs do not have the luxury of getting it totally wrong first time. The chances of cruising effortlessly through the SENIC phase are slim. After all, the survival statistics of entrepreneurial businesses don't lie. In a special report on family business[5] and chances of survival, the *Economist* stated,

> But in reality, very large numbers fail to make the leap. Only a third of businesses successfully make the transition from each generation to the next, says Mr. Astrachan[6]—"and that figure has been very stable, and is true around the globe." The majority are either sold or wound up after the founder's death. Some studies suggest that only 5% of family firms are still creating shareholder value beyond the third generation.[7]

Whether the generation leap triggers the first organizational crisis or other factors are responsible for it, arrive it will. So to reiterate, this is really a book about post-entrepreneurial businesses that have hit difficulties due to growth or have run out of steam. The main object of this book is to help entrepreneurs get beyond this SENIC phase and confidently enter a planned period of sustainable growth, in other words, to enhance your chances of success.

People Power

One thing this book can't do is give entrepreneurs instant advice on how to get more customers in a decreasing market, how to improve quality without considerable effort, or how to enhance logistics on a shoestring.

What this book can do is to help all the parties involved in SENIC businesses understand the very basic notion behind all organizational principles, which was so well put by Henry Ford in 1944: "You can take my factories, burn my buildings, but give me my people and I will build the business right back again."[8]

Ground Rules

All the examples given in the book are real, however bizarre they might sound, and often relate to my own experiences. If they are not incorporated in the text, then they are offered as short stories of the "It Couldn't Happen to You—or Could It?" variety. In short I will refer to these as *Time Outs*, as illustrated previously in Time Out 1.1. Time Outs do not form part of the main text. They are presented as independent anecdotes to illustrate a point or relate to an experience. Often they also present the light-hearted side of SENIC, but nevertheless with real consequences. Just because it's funny doesn't mean it was right or effective!

In order to protect the people involved and also, naturally, to keep the lawyers at bay, countries, business names, and names of owners and employees are disguised unless specifically referenced. That's the advantage of having worked in so many countries in a variety of industries. So if you as an entrepreneur or business owner or employee recognize yourself in the text, it is purely coincidental. The relevant text, without fail, will not, repeat *not*, refer to the SENIC business or circumstances that you are thinking about. Rather they refer to another business struggling and fighting with the same problems under similar circumstances in a faraway marketplace in one of those "foreign countries."

You'll find, after every section, the main points summarized. They are termed *Fouls* or *Free Throws*. Fouls are actions that can be avoided, but that will be penalized in the marketplace when they are not avoided. Free throws are just that—preemptive actions made without competitive pressure that can make the life of an entrepreneur so much easier.

The book also has some references to sport. In my opinion, business is like a game that needs to be played and enjoyed by all parties involved. Don't forget the "rule breakers" are often new businesses and the "rule makers" are the existing players desperately trying to protect their turf in the name of customer concerns, industry standards, or some other pretense often concocted by the lawyers or, even worse, government officials influenced by the industry leaders. Entrepreneurs and new businesses are the lifeblood of a free-market economy. Some of them will grow into the multinationals of the future because the existing multinationals will have run out of steam. If you don't believe that, look at the *Fortune* 500 of fifty years ago and see how many companies on that list are still active today. Not unlike products, organizations have life cycles, too.

So enjoy this book and take heed of the observations and implications. As I have always said, without fail, to all the players in every SENIC business that I had the pleasure to be associated with, "Never mind all that, the best is yet to come."

NOTES

1. Greiner, Larry E., "Evolution and Revolution as Organizations Grow," *Harvard Business Review* July–August 1972. A short note on the early part of a company's life cycle is given as Appendix A.

2. Reported on the Grant Thornton Web site at http:/67.96.180.115/fc_comm.asp under the heading "Family Culture." Published by Grant Thornton International, 2004.

3. The Peter Principle, based on a book by Dr. Lawrence J. Peter and Raymond Hull (1969), says that everyone gets promoted to his level of incompetence.

4. Passed along to me by Tony Factor, one of the most successful businessmen in South Africa during the 1980s and 1990s. He was dyslexic and used to encourage his staff by saying, "If I can do this, and I cannot read or write, then you can do it."

5. The distinction between entrepreneurial business and family business is somewhat blurred. However, consider that the majority of entrepreneurial businesses are family businesses. When an entrepreneurial business can be described as a family business is probably a moot point.

6. Joe Astrachan, Cox Family Enterprise Center, Kennesaw State University, Georgia, USA.

7. Special Report, "Family Businesses; Passing on the Crown," The *Economist* (November 4, 2004): 2.

8. From www.motivational-inspirational-corner.com/getquote.html?startrow=21 &authorid=8.

2

What Needs to Change and Why

Entrepreneur: Do I have to change, too?
Answer: Yes, that's the price of progress.

INTRODUCTION

Question: What are we playing?
Entrepreneur: Who cares—keep playing!

The creative period must seem a long time ago for any entrepreneur and his employees when the first revolutionary crisis hits them, sometimes without too much warning. The exhilarating days of creativity, long fruitful hours, and companionship appear to be a distant memory. And what's more, they are alas of little use to the current state of play.

SENIC Arrival

The inevitable crisis is a first but vital step on the challenging road to a company's future development. "No pain, no gain," so to speak. Naturally, in my experience, for each business this first crisis takes on a unique style and spans a different time frame. Gradual or sudden, induced or natural, kick or push started, it doesn't really matter. What matters is that the by-now SENIC organization (remember, Still Evolving, Now in Crisis) has achieved some measure of success, by hook or by crook, by design or luck, by hard plodding or dream walking, or any other way you can think of. In marketing speak, the business has created, or is filling, a significant need in the marketplace. Customers are buying its products or services. What's even more useful, they are paying for them!

Small businesses, such as the corner shop, the local tradesman, the local garage, and so forth, are examples of ongoing small organizations that are run, almost exclusively, by entrepreneurs or owner-managers. But the SENIC organizations that I am talking about have grown beyond the small businesses that fill local needs in well-defined niches for a limited geographical market.

Businesses that do arrive at the turbulent first revolutionary crisis period have respectable sales and have frequently grown beyond the local scene, probably employ a significant number of people, and have developed some hierarchy or pecking order, often determined by the length of service of the employees. But make no mistake about it, the entrepreneur still calls all the shots.

At this stage, most entrepreneurs have been to the short evening courses run by the Chamber of Commerce or have attended one of those expensive lectures by a famous management guru. They have started to think of renaming the business, re-branding its products, getting a mission and making a mission statement (why, I don't know), and figuring out what their market share could be. They are earnestly considering a major advertising campaign, trying to develop a master plan, and of course compiling a serious budget. Plans and budgets are what real business is all about, according to the numerous consultants they might already have employed.

SENIC businesses are purported to be more flexible. They react faster to what customers want and make instantaneous decisions. Whether this is true remains to be seen. Some of these businesses have survived already for a considerable length of time. But in organizational terms they are still only just past the entrepreneurial phase.

Nonetheless, warts and all, having achieved SENIC status is no mean feat for an entrepreneur and his business. Many such businesses do not make it beyond the first couple of years and business survival will be tested time and time again. In a recent article on longevity, the *Economist* reported as follows:

> What is clear is that corporate longevity is highly unusual. One-third of the firms in the *Fortune* 500 in 1970 no longer existed in 1983, killed by merger, acquisition, bankruptcy or break-up. According to Leslie Hannah, a business historian at the University of Tokyo, the average "half-life" of big companies—that is, the time taken to die by half of the firms in the world's top 100 by market capitalisation in any given year—was 75 years during the 20th century. *For small companies, most studies suggest a half-life in single figures. Corporate infant mortality is particularly high; the first year is the hardest.* [Emphasis added.][1]

Nothing particularly encouraging to look forward to, you might say. Fortunately, the average entrepreneur does not realize, or does not want to realize, what lies ahead. Otherwise, most of them would probably stay put and accept partial success. Having said that, it's probably much more likely that partial success is not an option for an entrepreneur, the ones I have known anyway. They have had a recent history of success and believe they always make the right decisions on gut feel. So without too much ado and almost without further thoughts or deliberations, these entrepreneurs took the next major hurdle and jumped into the unknown.

How to Follow Through

This hurdle is an even more daunting prospect than that presented by the start-up phase. The SENIC business will have to develop into a real organization.

In reality, this means that the old "come on let's get on with it" attitude no longer works, and opportunities and problems can no longer be addressed informally or even dynamically. More method and order is required to start performing consistently. The significant and more demanding customer base will settle for nothing less. The competition has noticed, too, and is starting to take the newcomer seriously. At this stage, most entrepreneurs realize that their trusted sidekicks can no longer cope with all the demands of the increased business. Adding more people, a salesperson here, an accountant there, and clerks everywhere, does not seem to help at all. It's almost a black hole because the new employees do not appear to understand the well-established, but to outsiders peculiar and unfamiliar, system. Time for real training is unavailable, so the confusion increases and the on-the-job training sessions are erratic. Much easier to do it yourself!

The realization that your team can't do everything and that you have to start practicing saying "no" to requests that are clearly beyond the scope of the SENIC organization's capabilities has not as yet been considered by some entrepreneurs. Almost ultimate flexibility is still practiced under the disguise of the slogans invented by the real giants of industry, such as, "You name it we do it," "No request is too small or too big for us," or "We have a can-do attitude around here."

The fact that these slogans only apply to the real capabilities of an organization seem to have gotten lost in translation. I have seen product offerings of medium-sized wholesale companies that would do proud to a Wal-Mart catalog. I have also seen extra-special orders for "new but promising" clients that required major modifications to plant and machinery with appalling set-up times that would make any production manager despair. And I've seen special deliveries to very small, way-out-of-town clients that seriously delayed major deliveries on a regular basis.

Typical SENIC Onset

The speedy or eventual arrival of a business at the first revolutionary crisis is often the result of one of the following:

1. The acquisition of the first really large contract.
2. Short-lived honeymoon after the first major contract.
3. A gifted entrepreneur gets too far ahead of the team.
4. A too-extreme focus on the truly innovative product (to the exclusion of organizational development).

The acquisition of the first really large contract can actually bring on a crisis. Sometimes a new client or customer acquisition is gained by undercutting the more established players and cajoling the client. How this is done in practice only the on-the-spot entrepreneur can tell. But believe me, there are no rules, prisoners are not taken, and we all know that bribes and backhanders are not allowed, so figure it out for yourself. This is a time for celebration, the champagne flows freely, the new, luxurious executive car has been ordered already, and now all the organization has to do is perform.

Alternatively, the first major contract might have been acquired some time ago but the honeymoon was short lived. Now everything seems to be going wrong. The new, more-demanding customer does not appear to have the patience of the established customer base. It expects contract performance. One entrepreneur that I was introduced to, and who at that moment lived this particular nightmare, said to me during our first meeting, "It's that endless thing about specifications, quality, and on-time delivery that drives you up the wall."

It is possible also that the growth was not achieved by one clean swoop, but by several spells of relentless and uncontrollable growth. For reasons beyond anyone's explanation, the business has hit a sweet spot in the market. The unexpected has happened; lady luck does exist but she has struck with a vengeance. The organization is unable to cope. Customer complaints are the order of the day and the chances are that the cash flow is thoroughly—with any luck not disastrously—out of control.

Of course there is always the exceptional, but in a sense unusually gifted, entrepreneur who can't be stopped. One I came across had realized that his particular pitch was highly successful and he started bringing in new clients like a fisherman on a lucky shore with the right bait. The organization was left more and more to its own resources. It was faltering and the business engine was starting to splutter, but this seemed to spur him on to even greater sales efforts. It was almost as if he wanted to prove that he could overstretch and break anything and anyone because of his sheer brilliance. He could not understand that his success, his determination, and his dedication were not transmitted to the rest of the organization. That's why it appeared, in his mind, to sabotage his superhuman efforts to keep growing. He started to ignore his own organization, did not want to understand why it couldn't cope, and even played with the idea of outsourcing, but the patience of his clients was running out and so was his cash flow.

Then there is the scenario of a genuine demand for an innovative product. An entrepreneur that had this well-deserved event befall him realized it, but for the life of him didn't know how to go about creating a business around it. He almost resisted the idea of financial success and was working on version two, three, and four before version one was fully tested and operational. Functioning somewhere between invention and production, his organization was never geared to exploit success and his inventor-biased employees were not geared for the day-to-day routine of production. Any excuse to start discussing the next updated version was grasped by all to the despair of the sales force. They couldn't understand why the factory never performed, was always late, and product quality was suspect. Some of the more established competitors started experimenting with similar products. The window of opportunity in such situations closes rapidly.

The previous examples might be extreme, but illustrate starkly, I trust, what is meant by "arriving at the SENIC stage." At this stage, quite a few entrepreneurs are probably advised by their accountants or legal advisors that a senior manager should be hired to "move the business along and to get a better grip on things." At first the common reaction of most entrepreneurs is one of disbelief and rejection. They often start working even longer hours and demand the same from their dependable core of employees. For a short while this might help, but unfortunately not for long. Working smarter is required, not working harder.

The by-now worn-out entrepreneur starts to think that his accountants or lawyers have a point. Being somewhat skeptical to most outside so-called business advice is in and of itself not a bad attitude to have in a world of hungry consultants. However, these professional advisors appear to have a distinct advantage: they are the only outsiders that the entrepreneur trusts explicitly. Like most consultants, the accountants and the lawyers can listen without interruptions and always show a degree of patience that mere mortals like me can only admire. But above all and anything else, they never contradict a client!

Unfortunately, in more instances than I care to remember, and as a result of their confidential business relationship, entrepreneurs appoint a lawyer or accountant—people who have never managed anything in their own lives—to head the selection process for one or more senior managers. It's an understandable chain of events, but not a great start to what ultimately must be solved: the first organizational crisis.

Challenges Ahead

For now, the SENIC business has reached the stage where it plays a not-insignificant part in the market. Competitors, if there are any, are starting to take note. Much larger organizations are considering how big the market for the novel product offering really is. Any organization, even at the SENIC stage, is bigger than one man or woman. But most of the credit for this desirable, but now also precarious, state of affairs can be credited to one person, and one person only—the entrepreneur. Yet now the challenge of the first organizational crisis needs to be overcome. Dedication, hard work, and informal communications will no longer suffice. The organization will have to change and all the players will have to adapt.

FOULS
- Dreaming and talking of "the good old days."
- Working harder all the time.
- Adding more and more bodies without structure.

- Not saying "no" to customers.
- Taking management advice from professionals who have never managed anything themselves.

FREE THROWS
- Look realistically at where the business is.
- Work smarter, not harder.
- Add structure before more bodies.
- Say "no" to customers.
- Seek management advice from successful managers.

DECIDE ON WHAT YOU WANT

Entrepreneur: Can't we just keep on going regardless?
Answer: No and no again! As Churchill once said, "This is not the End, it is not even the Beginning of the End, but it is the End of the Beginning."

What Do You Want?

This simple but central question will determine the course that the SENIC business will follow in order to start operating consistently and successfully. The answer to this question is not only important for the entrepreneur but also of critical significance to all other players, such as the employees, the clients, and perhaps even the entrepreneur's family.

Yes, as an owner of a business you have to decide what you actually want. If you don't know and you leave it to chance, making it up as you go along, the chances are that you end up where you don't want to be. As an entrepreneur your determination to get the business going was the only target. Now with some continuity achieved it is necessary to firm up on plans and goals and transmit these to your staff. You cannot expect existing and new employees to achieve the goals you might or might not have in your head.

Icarus Paradox

There are some dangers lurking, namely, past success can lead to both inertia and recklessness. Business success to date can lead to reluctance to change or even risk-aversion behavior. Contrarily, the same success can breed a sense of invincibility and promote reckless action. Ranft and O'Neill (2002)[2] refer to the latter as the "Icarus Paradox." Icarus, of course, is the mythical figure who was overconfident of his own powers and eventually fell back to earth after flying too close to the sun.

Both inertia and invincibility are options that will not be conducive to the current crisis of a SENIC business. So it is important to take a more structured approach and proceed with the critical issues one at a time, with or without the help of senior employees.

It Couldn't Happen to You—or Could It?
TIME OUT 2.1
Alice in Wonderland, or a Simple Strategy Riddle

Alice is walking along the brick road, not the yellow variety, which not too far ahead splits into two seemingly similar but diverging roads. At this junction stands a large tree, and spread out on one of the lower branches is the Cheshire cat. The following dialogue takes place between Alice and the Cheshire cat:

Alice: Where am I?
Cheshire cat: Where do you want to go?
Alice: I don't know.
Cheshire cat: Then it doesn't really matter where you are!

To answer the question, "What do you want?" it is always useful, even crucial, to first of all determine what the current state of play in the business is. In other words, where is it now?

Where Are You Now

A realistic and honest appraisal of the SENIC business's current health is required from as many sources as practicable. Talk to customers and find out what they think about the business. Listen to the sales force. It is always extremely enlightening to hear what customers say to them. Listen to new employees. At this stage, they are still the unbiased outsiders with a fresh and perhaps even simplistic look that can be very revealing. Give existing employees[3] the opportunity to voice their opinion on the present situation. Why is this input so important?

It is of vital importance because future success is only achieved through the people who work for the business and the clients it serves.

If the SENIC business is going through a bad phase and is losing money, the questions, "Where are you?" and "What do you want?" are just as relevant. Getting the business back to profitability might just lie in addressing the symptoms and not the cause of the problem(s) as yet. Although it is obviously essential to get the balance between income and expenditure back in favor of the first, avoid throwing out the baby with the bathwater. Also, make sure that in reducing employee costs to acceptable levels, the skills base in the current organization is not permanently damaged so that the business still has a fighting chance with the remaining employees. Just being left as entrepreneur with your original employees is acceptable surely as long as their skills are the required and necessary ones for your future adjusted plans. Be realistic and realize that the business has moved back on the development curve of its life cycle and that the first attempt at growth to reach the next phase has failed. Hopefully, as an entrepreneur, you have learned something. It is always better still to have tried and failed than not to have tried and lost the opportunity to succeed.

When you, as the entrepreneur, have a good feel for what the business's capabilities are today, you must return to the question, "What Do I want?" We are now entering the realm of setting strategy.

Setting Strategy

As the owner of the business, you cannot avoid the responsibility of strategy setting. You can get all the input you want, and use any number of strategy consultants to give you advice, but you cannot delegate the setting of the strategy. This would be an abdication of your authority, a passing of the buck to advisers who can walk away from it without any consequences whatsoever. After all, it is still your company.

Unfortunately, actually rather fortunately for you, no one can create a strategy for your unique business. As Gary Hamel (1977) wrote, "The dirty little secret of the strategy industry (all these consultants, gurus and planners) is that it doesn't have any theory of strategy creation. Whenever we come across a brilliantly successful strategy, we are all inclined to ask, 'Was it luck or was it foresight? Did these guys have this thing all figured out, or did they just stumble into success?'"[4]

Everyone is capable of recognizing a strategy after it has succeeded. We are all wise after the events have taken place and can elaborate at length on how it was achieved. The major point made here is that no outsider, in particular no consultant, can really help you with the creation of a strategy.

Planning Is Not Strategy

In contrast, consultants and all professional managers are trained pretty well in the process of planning. The only problem is that this process, useful as it may be, still does not produce strategy. Henry Mintzberg writes, "The popular way to address this problem [of strategy creation] has been to try to improve the implementation. 'Manage culture,' executives have been advised, or 'tighten up on your control systems.' A whole segment of the consulting industry has grown up to help organizations become better at implementation."[5]

But to concentrate on the planning process rather than to create a strategy is putting the cart before the horse. The effective implementation of a strategy surely depends on a clear strategy for starters. To force this creative process into a box labeled "set strategy" in order to complete the planning cycle is as useful as to be a very proficient pilot with no destination. If you don't know where you are flying to there's little point in taking off.

The argument I am making is this: Never, never force the strategy-creation process. Strategy setting cannot be dealt with in a few easy, planned-in-advance brainstorming sessions or by "setting the timetable for the planning cycle." If you do not have a strong vision for your business any longer, easy does it. Don't let anyone, and certainly not a consultant, drive you in a direction you don't want to go. Look at your current position with your existing management and staff and see how you can improve it without shaking the world. Just improve and be very good at what you are doing and who knows, the adjusted vision or strategy will hit you and your organization in the maturity of time.

Vision or Mission

If you do still have a strong vision for the business you need to share it with your management team. The point I made earlier is important, namely, the vision has to get out of your head and into the organization as the strategy. After all, the vision on its own is not enough. You need to seek and explore ways to realize that vision. But just because you are going through the SENIC phase should not distract you in pursuing your vision. It is rare enough for a SENIC business to have a strong vision!

A lot has been said and written in the popular management press on the mission and the mission statement. What the real practical difference is between a vision, a strategy, and a mission, I have not as yet discovered myself. So if there is a sensible difference I can't share it with you. What I do know is that even start-up and SENIC companies have been pressed into devising a mission statement or vision.

It is easy enough to make pronouncements like, "We strive to be the supplier of choice," "We will provide a service second to none," "Our customers are always right," and so forth. It is more difficult and it takes considerable dedication and energy to answer this question: How are you going to achieve this promise? What is more, are the employees aware that you take the mission statement seriously?

Mission statements, even from some of the very large businesses, do not address how this promise to customers will be realized. In practice, these statements are often nothing more than meaningless sentences totally at odds with actual practice. In their book on strategy, Mintzberg, Ahlstrand, and Lampel (1998) wrote: "Warren Bennis[6] perhaps put it best with the comment that 'if it is really a vision, you'll never forget it.' Wouldn't this make a wonderful test for all these banal statements labeled 'the vision'!"[7]

So don't spend months looking for the right mission statement. Just act and your customers will be the mission statement. They will tell you soon enough whether you are allowed to exist.

Another important point to consider is whether the existing business is the right vehicle for achieving what you want. In other words, if the business has disassociated itself from your vision, for whatever reason, do you see this new direction as a possible winner, or will you keep on trying to fit a square peg in a round hole?

This is not an easy question to answer, but again it needs to be considered seriously.

Next and last on the list of vital points that need to be addressed is the question, "If you know what you want, how will you get there?"

How?

This is where the planning process should take over and you ask detailed questions, such as:

- How do you propose to enter the new market?
- How do you envisage getting sales up by 25 percent?
- How are you going to finance the increase in working capital?
- How are you going to finance additional plants?
- How are you going to get overdue receivables back to thirty days?
- How are you going to reduce customer complaints by 15 percent?
- How will you get factory rejects to below 5 percent?
- Not to forget, how will you get the training or the human resources to execute the plans?

And so on and so forth. In other words this is the time for *how* questions and their proposed actions.

So let's recap. The three basic but vital questions that you as the entrepreneur should ask are:

1. Where are you now?
2. What do you want?
3. How can you get there?

These questions sum up the overall strategy process that must be developed for the SENIC business.

When there are answers for the *where* and *what* topics and action plans for the *how* questions have been developed, commit the strategy and the actions to paper. Paper has a sobering influence on ideas. It also indicates to your own organization that you are serious about the direction the organization is taking and the goals you want to achieve. Just because it's on paper doesn't mean it can't be changed. However, it does mean that any important change must again be investigated and officially incorporated.

KISS

Keep the written strategy and action document as short and simple as possible. The old adage KISS—Keep It Simple Stupid—should always apply. Particularly in today's fast-moving world, most employees skim. They find it difficult to concentrate beyond the first page or sometimes even beyond the summary, for that matter. We all suffer from data overload, and if you don't believe me, use my standard test for exposing this twenty-first century phenomenon. Send someone an e-mail with more than three questions imbedded in the text. Bet your boots you get an answer to only one of these questions in the reply e-mail, if you are lucky! The good old days of correct and well-thought-out correspondence are long since gone. Why do you think there are so many lawyers about?

Stick with the Knitting

When a SENIC business is really struggling, some entrepreneurs think of diversifying themselves out of trouble. Examples abound in the popular press of entrepreneurs who went from strength to strength in more than one business. Their conglomerates often comprised a series of businesses from hotels to manufacturing to insurance. These particularly gifted entrepreneurs are real exceptions and also have batteries of talented managers, familiar with each of the industries, to run their empire. Often, the inner workings of these empires are not known, and to what extent the one part supports the other is hidden in the overall result. If these empires will ever make a second or third generation, only time will tell, but remember the articles and statistics on the chances of survival quoted before.

Good advice for the SENIC phase is "stick to the knitting." In other words, don't try and improve your bottom line by diversifying away from your core business. Get the core business right before you even think of diversifying. You cannot get yourself out of a hole by starting to dig another one. Focus on the one you have and put it right. That's the message for a practical strategy.

FOULS
- Trying to diversify yourself out of trouble.
- Planning instead of setting a strategy.
- Not knowing where you are, what you want, or how to get there.

FREE THROWS
- Understand that your customers are the mission statement.
- Answer: "Where are you now?"
- Answer: "What do you want?"
- Answer: "How can you get there?"
- Answer the how questions before creating mission/vision/strategy statements.
- KISS.
- Stick to the knitting during SENIC.

YOUR CUSTOMERS ARE THE KEY TO GROWTH

The purpose of a business is to create a customer.

Peter Drucker

The heart and soul of any business are its customers. Without customers there is no business. The so-called customer services departments of some very large corporations often test this basic notion to its very core as we, the customers, are passed from choice to choice by means of an automatic answering mechanism that tries to determine what our problem is. When we eventually reach the end of the choices menu and a real person is supposed to take over, the soft music starts and we have to listen to that most famous of automatic messages, "All our operators are busy but please stay on the line, your call is important to us." That it's even more important to us seems to be of no concern to the powers to be. After all, we are trying to get some customer satisfaction and are paying for the call. Telephone companies must love this process of dialing the "help" line, making choices, pushing buttons, listening to soft music and that famous message.

As an entrepreneur you don't have to be told that the customer is important. Your whole entrepreneurial life and business has revolved around your very own home-grown customers. But now the SENIC phase has been reached and there are many internal measures required to facilitate growth. It's difficult to keep your entrepreneurial eye on the ball, implement internal changes, and at the same time keep your customers happy. Perhaps, it might be time also for a slightly more discerning approach to customers. The customer is still king, but who actually is the customer?

Who Is the Customer?

Post-entrepreneurial businesses in SENIC mode are often in trouble because their product lines are too varied and no one knows anymore which lines are making money and which lines don't. It is a good thing to listen to your customers and try and improve your product or service, but it is another thing to allow each and every customer the modifications or special conditions he demands. You can no longer afford to make every product a "once off." You, the post-entrepreneurial SENIC business owner, must become more aware of what you are truly offering the market place. That's another way of saying, "decide who you want your customers to be." That's not an easy decision, but it will have to be made in order to pass the SENIC stage successfully. Quite a few SENIC failures are recorded amongst growing companies with full but totally confused order books.

Shift in Customer Spectrum

Sometimes, your original customers, never mind how loyal they have been, need to be left behind in order to satisfy your newer customers with their larger order books. A classic example of this was an electrical contractor who inherited the business from his father with a loyal local clientele. The business's main emphasis was the installation and repair market for private houses. He employed about five electricians. Ambitious as he was, he kept on trying to penetrate the bigger league and eventually scored his first success on a big contract for the electrical installation of a new shopping mall. After having completed this contract successfully, he got the taste of success and started to concentrate on larger contracts. Although he tried to keep his original customers, they were unhappy because he couldn't provide the same friendly neighborhood service that they were used to. He now employed 28 electricians, and a few people in the office. His customer spectrum had shifted and he could no longer afford to mix the old with the new. He tried for quite some time to keep everyone happy, at considerable cost to his business, but all he did was prolong the SENIC phase.

Key Customers

Thus, if you can no longer satisfy all your customers with your limited resources, that is, production capacity, financial constraints, and so forth, it is time to consider a *key customer* approach. In other words there are customers and there are customers. Look at your sales numbers[8] and rank customers according to turnover size. Consider other parameters, such as, payment history, delivery issues, growth potential, or any other topics that you think are of importance to your ranking system—no more than five parameters. Now rank your customers. It sounds tough, but tough decisions have to be made. Then organize your business so that these key customers are serviced as best you can. After all, they will form the basis of SENIC survival and future growth.

"Polar" Scenarios

Let's also discuss some cases at the extremes of the customer spectrum. There are a lot of post-entrepreneurial companies whose income is almost totally dependent on one customer. Unless you are supplying something very special or are tied in to your sole major customer by some sort of unique sole supplier agreement, you will no doubt agree that your SENIC business is very vulnerable. Your customer, more than likely much larger than your business, has you where it hurts most and is probably already looking for possible alternate suppliers. The unspoken rule in a lot of large organizations is: get 80 percent of your requirements for a particular product from supplier A and 20 percent from supplier B so you keep them both on their toes and the organization cannot be held to ransom. The message for you, the entrepreneur is, keep this sole customer deliriously happy, but make it your mission to look for additional customers.

The other extreme is the post-entrepreneurial business that has hundreds if not thousands of customers, probably individual consumers—not unreal in the e-commerce era for service type products. If you have this sort of

It Couldn't Happen to You—or Could It?
TIME OUT 2.2
Sometimes You Gotta Let them Go to Keep Them

This particular example relates to a specialized building products manufacturer. The owner/entrepreneur of this company had built his business quite successfully over a period of six years in a market that was focused on price and delivery. One of the major customers of the business had a particularly awkward job that would add at least 20 percent to the manufacturing and installation costs of a relatively standard item. Standard Pricing levels were around $28 to $30 per meter installed and we had asked for a premium of $4 per meter to cover the additional production and installation costs. The client was adamant that he was not going to pay more than $27.50. We knew that at that price it would be a real challenge to make any money at all, given the additional "once off and never before done" production requirement and the more than challenging delivery times. We also knew that there were two competitors dead keen to get the job and establish a relationship with our customer. We had a well-above-average rating from the client for quality and delivery. The strategy we decided upon went as follows: we decided to keep negotiating and make sure the price would end up below $29. We "passed" at around $29 by informing the client that for this particular job we unfortunately could no longer be considered, and we let the other two fight it out. Eventually one of them got the contract at around $28. We could watch with great satisfaction as one of our competitors messed up, particularly on delivery. The extra production and installation work had not been properly evaluated and, what's much worse, priced in the quest to score with a new client. The client was hitting him with additional charges like they were going out of fashion, and the contract became a nightmare scenario for both our competitor and the client. We kept good contact with the client but never mentioned this particular contract. We didn't have to because the client kept on complaining about his relationship with the new producer. We listened politely but retained a neutral pose. Needless to say, when the next contract from this client came along we were in with a much-better-than-average chance with our reputation of sound production and delivery intact. "Sometimes you gotta let them go to keep them."

business you must try and stay ahead of the competition by being inventive and competitive and being very much aware of what the consumer wants and the overall market offers. What you acquired in droves will also leave in droves if you are not careful.

Of course the ultimate scenario is a well-balanced portfolio of clients that are spread across a number of unrelated industries. That's the theory, but in practice you are probably tied to a particular industry and have to seek diversification within the industry.

Back to Basics

So again, who are your customers? There is no easy answer to this question, but a good starting point is to define a customer as someone who buys your product and pays for it (on time would be nice too, considering your strained cash flow during SENIC times). Thus, in a sense we are right back to the magic question posed in the previous chapter, "What do you want?" It does show that strategy and customers are very closely related. And why shouldn't they be? After all, customers are the heart and soul of your business.

Inverse Marketing

Strictly speaking *inverse marketing* does not belong in a chapter on customers. However, if I would have labeled it by its more common name, *procurement practices*, quite a few entrepreneurs would have skipped this part of the book. The entrepreneurs that I have known prefer to concentrate on customers, and quite rightly so. But please bear with me and consider this little diversion on inverse marketing as a critical part of seeking solutions to SENIC conditions.

The principle of inverse marketing starts with the observation that for some other companies, namely, your suppliers, you are the customer. They, suppliers to your business, are using the same marketing and sales techniques that you are using with your customers. Thus it stands to reason that if you do not pay enough attention to the manner in which your company makes its purchases, you will be considered a "slam dunk" by quite a few of your suppliers. In other words, they are maximizing their return at your expense. Now here comes the most valuable observation about practicing inverse marketing, namely, every dollar saved in purchasing goes straight to your bottom line. That certainly is a well-known, but often forgotten, fact that is particularly interesting to companies during the SENIC phase. To get an extra dollar to your bottom line via sales requires a whole series of actions for your company, such as, sales, manufacturing, distribution, and so forth. But again, there is absolutely no dilution from a dollar that you can save on purchasing. Once you are ready not only to acknowledge this fact but also to act upon it, you are ready for the discipline of inverse marketing.

Inverse marketing is nothing else than realizing that you can counteract the salespeople of your suppliers by some simple rules. Argue, let them sweat, negotiate the whole package—price, quality, delivery times, payment conditions, and so forth. Now *you* are the customer and you should be in the driving seat.

Most SENIC businesses are much smaller than the suppliers that provide them with the necessary raw materials. Nevertheless, try and find out how important you are to your suppliers. If possible find suppliers that are about your size. They are anxious to get ahead and will often give you better service and keener prices. Remember, you are doing the same for your own customers in order to grow. This is your business game but in reverse. Grab the wheel and enjoy the ride!

Concentrate first on your major purchases. If at all possible, get agreements on price and quantity with some sliding price scale according to quantity purchased. Then move down. Save money on items that everyone is too busy to pay attention to, such as your packaging, stationary, office supplies, and so forth. It's amazing what can be saved if you shop around. And keep on reminding yourself that purchasing is marketing/sales in reverse with an added advantage of, "a dollar saved is a dollar earned." That's inverse marketing.

Dealing with Complaints

To get a genuine complaint about your product or your service is not nice at all. It's a very sobering thought for most entrepreneurs to realize that they are not perfect. There are plenty of books available that will tell you how to deal with customer complaints. They make it sound so easy. Just follow the ten steps and you will have made a friend, that is, a faithful customer, out of a potential enemy. Particularly the inevitable step called "fix the problem" falls in a similar category to the one that was discussed in this chapter's Section "Decide on What You Want," with the box labeled "set strategy" as part of the planning process. Unfortunately the majority of real-life complaints of any substance are not rectified by being polite, thanking the customer for complaining, and giving him a token or a credit note. Remember the help line example quoted previously.

Having said all that, it is also true that a serious complaint presents a real opportunity to let the customer know what type of business you run. Sometimes from the ashes of a disaster will grow a long lasting business relationship built on the fact that you resolved an issue that was of great concern to a client. You probably learned something about your own product offerings as well. Maybe the client has pinpointed an internal weakness that you can eliminate, or perhaps he has found a flaw in what you thought was a perfect product. I know it's difficult but be thankful for complaints; you should discuss every significant complaint with your own people and give feedback to the client. Tell the client what you are going to do to put it right. Then try and avoid repeat performances. That's certainly one of the steps that will get you beyond the SENIC stage.

An example comes to mind of a small, project-based, manufacturing business with its own delivery trucks that I was associated with some time ago. Delivery of products to the only key customer was a problem due to its erratic order pattern and our own production lead times. In hindsight, both companies were well into SENIC and badly in need of some sort of planning tool. Both the manufacturer and the client had absolutely no room to store buffer stock to resolve the endless cycle of late deliveries, angry phone calls, charges and countercharges, until we hit on an idea. We located a small transport company that had no problem storing our products for our customer on its premises. This transport company became part of the loop. We, the manufacturing outfit, discontinued our own transport and all three parties were happy for a minimal increase in cost.

It's not always that easy. Every so often it just doesn't work and you must admit failure. If you can't put it right, say so. Then look for a solution that will limit the damage at, naturally, your expense. Honesty will at least get you the respect of what might become an ex-customer for the time being. Sometimes you just have to admit that the client and you were not the fit that you both expected. Better to admit it and move on than to prolong the agony. You can't fit a square peg in a round hole. Limit the damage and move on. At least your up-front approach will be remembered, and in business, you never know. After all, you are in there for the long run and what goes around comes around.

Customer Care

Now let's get back to the customers and looking after them. Looking after a customer means different things to different people in different businesses. But in general it means keep in contact and listen. Just because they order regularly, pay on time, and do all the wonderful things we expect from an ideal customer doesn't mean they don't deserve our attention. We all tend to spend time with customers who have complained, rightly or wrongly, or potential customers who we are trying to get into the fold. You also need to make sure you spend time with your faithful customers and realize that one of those is worth a hundred potential customers. The strength of the bond will get you to the position that even if the ever-faithful customers are considering changing, due to your price, your delivery problems, and so forth, they will come to you first and give you a chance to improve your ways.

If you have the chance, "infiltrate" your customer's organization at various operational levels. Let some of your employees meet and talk with some of theirs. Regular "face to face" averts a hundred e-mails and encourages cooperation in what are often common problems. But above all, make sure you deliver on your promises. Get a reputation for being a consistent and trustworthy supplier—that's an essential part of customer care. But don't forget, first of all, determine who your customers are. That's where it must start and that's where it should continue.

FOULS
- Trying to be "everything to everyone."
- Forcing a square peg into a round hole.

FREE THROWS
- Know who your customers are.
- Listen to your customers.

- View customer complaints as opportunities.
- If circumstances demand it, decide on key customers.
- Remember that good customers pay the bills!
- Don't forget: inverse marketing.
- Remember to keep good contact with quiet but regular customers.
- "Infiltrate" your customer's organization.

YOUR STAFF IS A CLOSE SECOND

Alone we can do so little: together we can do so much.
Helen Adams Keller (1880–1968)

Inner Circle

Each organization is only as good as the people that work for it. Everyone I know will agree with this truism. Another saying, quoted less frequently, goes like this: When circumstances change, people often can't change with them. In other words, an employee that was totally dedicated to you, the entrepreneur, and worked long hours with you during the creative period, does not necessarily make a good senior manager when the business requires one later on. Coupled with this, entrepreneurs often make poor choices in recruiting personnel. They tend to employ people that are fun to have around rather than those that get the work done.

In every SENIC business I have been in contact with, there was always a small inner group of people that liked the idea of working for the budding entrepreneur because of their previous connection with him. This relationship could have been based on a number of extended situations, such as, a previous working connection, a sport club, even old school ties, or the army—nothing like two years of compulsory boredom to foster lasting links—and so on. Somehow or other the bond was there and it obviously generated enough trust to accept working for you, the promising business owner in the making. Particularly during the start-up phase, it is not uncommon for these employees of the first hour, let's call them the *inner circle*, to be asked to do just about everything and anything. Only people who have the bond with the entrepreneur, and who don't mind trying their hand at all things learned and unlearned will survive.

Most entrepreneurs do not realize that the very first employees will set the tone for the company in years to come. These inner-circle employees are sometimes referred to as the "DNA" of the company. Unfortunately, the employment of relatives, friends, and other associates based on the "fun to have around" factor, without due concern for their suitability for the job at hand, will not enhance the chances of success. To put it more bluntly, these initial recruitment shortcomings are often the most predictable way to enhance failure in the future.

Outer Circle

If the start-up business is labor intensive, the rank and file will swell quite dramatically. However, our concern is primarily with the people who occupy supervisory roles. So at one stage or other, the need will be found to introduce some more management in the organization, a second echelon so to speak. Let's call these the *outer circle* employees. Because most entrepreneurs know damned well that recruitment is not their real forte, they gladly delegate the recruitment of additional supervision to their trusted, compliant, and very hard-working co-workers in the inner circle.

At this point, a very common human failing will surface. The inner circle proudly and jealously guards its recently acquired senior status. They do not want to be usurped by some cocky newcomer who might possibly know more than they do. So the chances are good to excellent that the inner circle will end up appointing candidates for outer-circle supervisory jobs who do not challenge them. As the inner-circle employees were probably recruited on their "fun to work with" factor rather than their management potential, they were never trained in supervisory skills.

Therefore, the second echelon, the outer-circle employees, have no chance! They learn from their mentors whatever wisdom is to be acquired. In the land of the blind, a one-eyed man is king. The expression, "We run a very flexible and dynamic outfit here," almost becomes the creed of the SENIC business. When you, the entrepreneur, hear this exciting and stimulating expression, please be forewarned. What the inner circle actually means is, "Every day is utter chaos around here. We don't like it, but we are used to it and don't know how to change it."

Most outer-circle employees stay with the program because they often don't know any better. I have heard outer-circle, junior supervisors in the year 2004 refer to a 1990s order-entry system, updated umpteen times by the IT contract person who was a friend of a brother of the entrepreneur, as that "fantastic order-entry system that tells you exactly what you need to know." It must be really nice to know what you need to know.

Inner and Outer Circle

The two groups of supervisory levels are different, but need each other because the way they have developed their work and routines is quite unique to the particular business. That is why, for example, Mr. X, the controller, an inner-circle member, is continually asked, "How do you cancel an order again?" Because to cancel an order requires an intimate knowledge of all the bits and pieces that were added to the original computer system. After a major and protracted display of keyboard skills, the outer-circle employee has renewed respect for Mr. X. After all, to repeat his keyboard gymnastics is almost impossible, particularly because not every order can be cancelled like that. There is still so much to learn!

The real problem is about to hit the business if it requires more skilled or supervisory personnel. Then the SENIC business will need a third type of manager, one with real management skills.

Real Recruitment

The personnel person, normally an inner-circle, upgraded secretarial assistant, or even worse, the finance and administration manager, is put in charge of the recruitment drive for new talent as the in-house recruiter. As this person has no extra time at all (because in a dynamic environment you have no time for these things), that person employs a recruitment consultant. What the person doesn't realize is that countless hours will now have to be spent on the "job specifications and how it fits into the organization" routine. The inner-circle personnel person never thought of that, because after all, "all we need is more help."

Alas, the recruitment consultant needs the fees, so to move the process along, she concocts a document of twenty pages with a few beautiful diagrams and a business doctrine that explains in many varied ways that new employees need to know that they will be joining a dynamic environment, and that their flexibility and adaptability to challenging circumstances, therefore, must be paramount. The consultant knows that no one in the organization, including you, the entrepreneur, will read the brief anyway—no one has the time or the inclination—and the recruitment process is begun.

The one thing a recruitment consultant knows is how to interview. So some good candidates are pre-selected and introduced to the business. The first interviews by the inner-circle personnel person assisted by the recruitment consultant are an education in itself. It is not uncommon that this type of interview is a one-man show. The in-house recruiter will give an hour-long lecture to the candidate on how he and his boss, that's you, the entrepreneur, developed the business to what it is now. Having suitably impressed the candidate with his "management weight" and interviewing skills, he will encourage the recruitment consultant to add to his confidence. The conversation goes something like this:

> "How did you think that went?" asks the inner circle recruiter. "I think, that went rather well," replies the recruitment consultant. Then, almost as an afterthought, she adds, "Do remember, though, to ask the next candidate about his experiences with Widgets Ltd. and Sunshine Plc?"

Even a recruitment consultant hungry for her fee has some standards!

The poor inner-circle personnel person is allowed to stumble along. In his mind, he has just heard confirmation that he is an excellent interviewer with a sharp sense of who is right for the business.

When final selection time comes around, the skillful recruitment consultant will have observed the one-man show ad nauseam and knows without fail the candidate our in-house recruiter likes by the latter's renewed enthusiasm in telling the "business saga," and his facial expressions, butt shifting, and nervously eager reactions. So the skillful recruitment consultant, if asked, will say, "I think Mr. 'YouLikeHimSoMuch' did rather well." This would confirm the in-house recruiter's excellent choice and professionalism and a decision is made. The recruitment consultant gives a sigh of relief. She will get her fees. After many reminders I might add, because suddenly, 25 percent of first-year salary not only sounds like a lot of money—it *is* a lot of money!

So now, a new bunch of supervisors will join the fray. Remember, the business is at a level or in a situation in which real supervisory skill is needed. Often these employees have worked for some years, probably for a larger business, and know a thing or two about supervisory skills, employee participation, management by objectives, conflict resolution, employee motivation, working conditions, and working hours.

They are in for the shock of their lives.

This group of employees is the first group that seriously starts to query some of the goings on in a SENIC business. Their loyalty bias is to their career, and to them could apply the crude statement, "If you want loyalty get a dog." Make no mistake, they are good at their jobs, they are hardworking, and they know their chosen field or profession. What's more, they are used to being involved in exchanges of ideas in the workplace. However, they are not compliant, do not shun an argument, and love to be involved in making decisions.

The first serious clashes of wills start occurring. The new supervisors recognize authority all right, but with them you have to earn it. Demanding respect won't get you anywhere. The idea of earning respect is a new concept for the inner-circle employees and their outer-circle protégés. Predictably enough, you the entrepreneur get the respect because of your entrepreneurial aura. Somehow or other your moods, antics and, let's face it, somewhat dictatorial manner are related to this, accepted and tolerated.

The problem sits with the inner-circle management and to a lesser extent with the outer circle add-ons. These employees find themselves in awkward situations trying to explain the (for them) logical way of doing business tasks in a particular way. If the new employees start to challenge these accepted work routines and procedures, the inner-circle management reverts to a well-known and familiar style, used by inexperienced managers that have no real answer to a question, by saying, "because I say so."

The outer-circle management is well used to this and has accepted it. Nevertheless they find it rather novel that someone could actually query an inner-circle manager. The new supervisors don't necessarily accept the "just do it" routine and want further explanations. They refer to previous experience and that further frustrates the inner circle.

It Couldn't Happen to You—or Could It?
TIME OUT 2.3
Life's a Stage and Recruitment Is the Scene

As someone who has had many assignments for SENIC companies, I have been interviewed quite a lot. Invariably, interviews with entrepreneurs are all about listening to the entrepreneur expound on his ideas and his life's work. Listening is not typically one of the virtues of entrepreneurs.

Scene I. One particular interview comes to mind. I was introduced to the entrepreneur who offered me a cup of coffee and asked me if I wanted milk and sugar. These were the only two questions that he asked me during the whole interview. I did try and interrupt a few times but to no avail. All in all I had to listen to the one-man show for over an hour. Afterwards I heard that he really enjoyed talking to me and that he was quite impressed with my qualifications and experience!

Scene II. The brother of an entrepreneur, let's call him Rupert, gainfully employed, sort of, as marketing manager in this particular SENIC business, once told me with great surprise and innocence that Mr. X, whom I had to fire for incompetence and laziness, had interviewed so well with him. As I knew that Rupert was a great "one man show" interviewer, I asked him what had swayed him in particular. Apparently Mr. X had told Rupert that he had never failed in the past and had made no plans to fail in the future!

Contract, Then Expand Again

The result of these conflicts is what I call the Expand-Contract phenomenon. This reflects the continuous effort to expand the management base, which is almost invariably and inevitably followed by an equivalent contraction due to dissatisfaction by the last group of supervisory-level employees, the expand-contract ones. They are willing to leave and change jobs if the environment and/or conditions are not to their liking.

The "if you can't get respect, you settle for fear" principle no longer has the desired effect. A new round of recruitment is started and the process repeats itself. Good people come in, then leave. In short, the expand-contract phenomenon strikes again. Particularly if the SENIC business books increased successes in the marketplace, it leads without fail to tremendous strains that are absorbed by inner- and outer-circle employees who start working longer and longer hours. Efficiency and often quality decreases even further. The training of new employees in the marvels and mysteries of the work system suffers accordingly and results in more and more exceptional circumstances, confusion, delays, re-works, irate customers, manual solutions to system problems, and so forth.

The sad part is that this particular phenomenon, Expand-Contract, experienced during the post-entrepreneurial phase and hence the first organizational crisis, is totally self-inflicted and almost never recognized by you, the entrepreneur, and your faithful band of inner- and outer-circle employees. You feel lost and demand more and more of your inner and outer circles. They seek another round of recruitment for additional supervision. Home and hobby life for these much-maligned but ever compliant employees is non-existent[9] and what has remained of the expand-contract group starts looking for another job. They want a career, not a vocation.

So often without even realizing it, you, the entrepreneur, can create chaos by delegating something, the recruitment process, to someone, an inner-circle employee, because you know that you weren't the right person to make the decision in the first place!

Table 2.1 summarizes my own experience with employees in SENIC businesses.

Now as an entrepreneur you might say, "That's all very nice, but how else could I have done it?"

To that I say, "Remember that you are not at SENIC for nothing. The very essence of the first organizational crisis is the word *organizational*." Mistakes have to be made, otherwise you have not grown sufficiently to experience them! Solutions will have to be found for the present and the future. The past is the past and no one can change it anymore. All we can do is learn from it. As an entrepreneur try and encourage challenges to the present situation, but above all listen. Your personnel are your greatest asset if, and only if, the right people are in the right job. The "band of brothers" that started with you is not necessarily the setup that gets you

Table 2.1
SENIC Business Management Employee Characteristics

	Loyalty	Flexibility	Compliancy	Management Skills
INNER CIRCLE	Greater love hath no man.	You name it, we do it.	Without the slightest hesitation.	Owner-manager inspired and also self-taught.
OUTER CIRCLE	Yes, because we don't know any better.	We aim to please most of the time.	Reluctantly.	Learned from INNER CIRCLE.
EXPAND-CONTRACT	Yes, but do we have to?	Are we capable of doing that?	Dares to differ.	Based on accepted and taught principles.

beyond SENIC. They are often part of the problem and will need to be evaluated as to their management potential and continued seniority in your business.

FOULS
- Continuing past recruitment practices.
- Pretending to enjoy "flexible and dynamic" environments.
- Accepting self-fulfilling prophesies transmitted by consultants.
- Experiencing the Expand-Contract phenomenon.
- Permitting unproductive long work weeks by inner- and outer-circle employees.

FREE THROWS
- Consider moving inner-circle personnel out of key positions.
- Make room for professionally trained managers.
- Understand that "the way you've always done it" may look like sheer lunacy to new employees.

CASH FLOW, THE ENGINE OF GROWTH

Accounting is a great system to record the past. Budgets are an effective system to control expenditure and to show that you have missed your far too optimistic sales forecasts once again. But cash flow is the only system that tells you "Where you are at" while making you continually think about the future with clammy hands.

The Author to an Entrepreneur (1995)

The Budget

To start a section on cash flow with the budget is somewhat misleading but done intentionally. The budget is often the only item left in SENIC businesses that is supposed to translate the mission or vision into action. The "myth of the revered budget" lives on. During SENIC phases, I have encountered entrepreneurs who convinced themselves that next year's sales budget was realistic and achievable. But how it was to be achieved remained a closely guarded secret even for the sales force. The spreadsheet exercise showed that if sales of X were achieved and expenditure was contained at Y, the business would be out of the red in no time. Needless to say, spreadsheets are a very powerful and tolerant tool to show what can be achieved if certain financial scenarios will take place. Unfortunately sales budgets are not as easy to control as expense budgets, and it is the sales side that really requires the famous "HOW" questions, discussed in Section

"Decide on What You Want," to overcome the "hope for the best" sales forecasts.

Every time I have been introduced to a new SENIC business and its entrepreneur(s), one of the first discussion items on the agenda was always the budget—not the vision, mission, or strategy, nor the various action plans, nor the marketing campaign or the sales drive, nor the personnel and operational capabilities, but always the budget. It was almost like these entrepreneurs felt that to control the budget was the solution to the overall problem. The financial forecast or budget is a vital part of the planning process and is an essential tool to translate and complement the strategy financially. It is not a substitute for strategy, although it is often the only document in the SENIC business vaguely related to a strategy. Without a sound strategy and action plans, the budget is just another spreadsheet exercise that your team ignores or uses when it suits them. Have it, by all means, but realize its limitations if it is a standalone document devoid of action plans.

Financial Control

Another myth that needs to be dispelled is the "myth of the ultimate control" exercised by withholding payment at the final stage of the purchasing cycle. To exercise control on payments, you need to control purchases at the stage of ordering. Make sure that your business has some form of control, exercised by you or your senior people, on what, when, and how to order supplies. That's where expenditure should be controlled—namely, before the expense is incurred. To withhold payment when goods and services have been delivered and sometimes consumed already is just delaying the inevitable. It might give you, the entrepreneur, a feeling of control, but the real control should have been exercised at the ordering stage. Withholding payment because you want to teach your employees that you exercise control is pseudo-control. It only gives you a bad name with your suppliers who, in turn, might frustrate your whole internal processes by delaying deliveries or even refusing to deliver. If you can't pay because of some temporary setbacks, something your cash flow should indicate, tell them and let them know when you can pay. This honest, up-front approach will get you sympathy and perhaps some consideration. Every business large and small has gone through difficult periods—that you can be assured of.

Cash Flow

To control the financial side of your SENIC business, it is much better to concentrate on cash flow—not the accounting variety, but the simple cash-in cash-out type. Do it in great detail, on a weekly basis if necessary, and involve as many senior managers as required. The financial controller can be the facilitator and the producer. She will try and sneak in non-cash items, such as depreciation or pre-payments, but don't allow that. The

It Couldn't Happen to You—or Could It?
TIME OUT 2.4
About Budgets, Check Books, and Ultimate Control

The organization in question had grown quite considerably in the last few years to about two hundred people spread out over five sites. At the time of my introduction, sales were very healthy, profit was made, and a sixth site was contemplated. Although the financial controller had managed to introduce some semblance of a payment system by means of purchase-order forms, employee working hours lists and the like, the two entrepreneurs, equal partners and both still very active in the business, exercised the ultimate control by being the only two authorized to sign checks.

This was normally done every Friday, and the exercise was dreaded by the financial controller. Frequently, up to 250 payments would have to be made. The two owners would ask all sorts of questions and would refuse to sign certain checks if in their eyes the answers given were not satisfactory. As the financial controller was seldom the initiator of a purchase or an expense, the poor fellow had to rely on the information obtained from various staff members spread out over five sites. This in turn led to further complications because checks not signed would often lead to non-delivery of ordered materials required by the business. This in turn would result in production delays, a frantic search for both entrepreneurs to explain the problem and get the check in question signed anyway, hand delivery of the check to the supplier's offices, and so forth.

A further complication was that there was as yet no management hierarchy and the sites were managed by a number of inner-circle employees.

The two owners suggested that I compile a budget as soon as possible, because they were pretty sick of what they called the "Fingerprint Routine" on a Friday as well. When I explained to them that we would have to develop the budget in tandem with the organization by determining who is responsible for what, they paid no attention. They just said, "get on with it." This was in my early days, so off I went, designing the organization, finding suitable candidates for positions, lecturing on responsibility and authority, discussing with the financial controller how we could keep it practical to get everyone involved, committed, and used to it, and in the meantime the Friday routine kept going strong. The only difference was that I was now involved as well, trying to explain why certain expenditures had been incurred and listening to constant remarks of expenditure being out of control and no one caring.

After a couple of months, we were ready. Proudly, I presented the new management team, elaborated on their responsibilities and authorities, and of course also submitted the chart of authorities. The financial controller then started presenting the budget, which was broken down by site and major spending categories. Some of this information had to be kept on "off-line" spreadsheets as the existing accounting system was creaking and we were in the process of looking for a replacement.

Suddenly one of the owners interrupted and asked, "But where can I find out how much coffee and tea is used by each one of the canteens?" Somewhat taken aback—remember, it was in my early days—I started to explain that we were not yet contemplating that type of detail because we wanted to let everyone get used to the system first before we detailed the budget further—also, that some of this detail was the responsibility of the budget holder. That was the wrong thing to say! The whole group got an hour-long tirade about loose spending habits, spending his and his partner's money, not caring, how they had not built the business for us so we could freely spend their hard earned cash, and so forth.

Unfortunately for everyone, the Friday sessions continued, because that is how the owners "felt" they really had control. The sessions became easier because I got a better grip on expenditure, and the management team did take its responsibilities seriously. But if one of the owners felt like it, he still did not sign a check for an expense incurred that was due for payment.

advantage of the simple cash-in cash-out variety is that non-financial managers start recognizing what really counts, namely, customers that pay on time and critical expenditure that has to be paid when due to keep your business ticking over. For example, it's a great eye opener for salespeople to appreciate the fact that a customer is only a "real" customer when he pays

It Couldn't Happen to You—or Could It?
TIME OUT 2.5
It's the Cash Flow, Stupid

This business operated in a contract environment. With lots of subcontractors to be paid on a regular basis, cash flow was particularly important. When I had been with the business for about a week, the head office was raided by Internal Revenue inspectors who had reason to believe that tax evasion had taken place on several occasions. The consequences of this accusation were the withdrawal of the tax-exempt certificate of the business. In practice this meant that every customer would have to withhold tax at the rate of about 40 percent from all our due payments, while our own payments to subcontractors, most of them with tax-exempt certificates, had to be made in full.

Now maybe this would not have been a problem in an industry with large profit margins, but in contracting at that time and in that particular country, margins were more in the region of 2 to 5 percent of the contract

(Continued)

sum. The business had also just taken on its biggest contract ever, so our difficulties were multiplied. Naturally, the owner and I spent a lot of time getting the affairs of the company in order with the Revenue Commissioners, but that is not the theme of the story.

Within a week of these happenings, the financial controller and I had set up a simple but effective cash flow system of the cash-in and cash-out variety. Every week, but sometimes more frequently, we would get information from the various sites when payments were due and when subcontractors or suppliers critical to a stage of the contract had to be paid. The bankers of the business were helpful as well, at a price naturally, and even the Internal Revenue dealt very quickly with our tax refunds after we had shown them that we had instituted procedures to eliminate all wrongdoings. All personnel, the owner included, became very efficient in collecting monies due and we also became artists in drawing out payments. For me, this was the epitome of cash-flow control. Personnel at all levels were involved and everyone learned very quickly that cash flow was the engine that kept the business going.

by involving them in the money collection routine. The argument that you can't engage salespeople in getting payment because "it would spoil their relationship with the client" does not hold water. Getting paid is an essential part of selling, and the sooner everyone in your business realizes it, the better. Managers responsible for expenditure, a production manager, for example, must also get involved. It's a great education for them as well and will make them much more discerning spenders. After all, their salaries are at stake!

Particularly when times are tough, an emphasis on liquidity rather than profits and budgets helps SENIC businesses overcome the problems of strained financial resources, lack of trained personnel, and a short-range management horizon imposed by an unpredictable competitive environment (Welsh and White, 1981).[10] An example of a straightforward but effective operational cash flow document with some explanatory notes is provided in Appendix C.

FOULS
- Believing in the Myth of the Budget
- Believing in the Myth of Ultimate Control

FREE THROWS
- Never mind the budget, concentrate on the cash flow.
- Make sure people know that cash flow is everyone's business.

SYSTEMS NEED TO BE ENHANCED

A system is a network of interdependent components that work together to try to accomplish the aim of the system. A system must have an aim. Without the aim, there is no system.

W. Edwards Deming (1900–1993)

The ways in which SENIC businesses deal with all types of data are as varied as the industries, organizations, and entrepreneurs that are out there. So, it is not my intention to discuss systems in SENIC businesses in their entirety. Nevertheless, some discussion on systems that are employed at this stage of the development of your company can be helpful. Systems don't make the business but they can sure stifle even a small company by their sometimes insatiable demand for data.

Critical Success Factors (CSFs)

To get beyond SENIC requires a focus on the Critical Success Factors (CSFs) of your business. As the name implies, Critical Success Factors are elements of your business that decide whether you live or die. As the entrepreneur, you should know what they are for your business. The monitoring of these should be the main priority of your business systems. In the end though, even systems are about people. You and your employees can use or abuse any system that you chose to introduce. There are no bad systems, only "badly used" or "not fit for purpose" systems.

Yet Again, "The Budget"

One thing most entrepreneurs I have ever known had, or wanted to have if they hadn't, was a budget. Somehow, this must have given them the secure feeling that they exercised a measure of formal control over their organization. The budget was often compiled by the financial controller[11] based on last year's actual numbers with a percentage increase for inflation. Operating departments were seldom consulted.[12] I have even encountered budgets generated by the external accountants of SENIC businesses. Almost like remote control, budgets in SENIC businesses tend to be exceedingly heavy on expenditure checks and light on the difficult stuff like sales forecasts. It is also not uncommon for some of these businesses to have an inordinate, almost horrendous number of expenditure categories.

Now it probably is not surprising that the entrepreneurs have little interest in accounting and accounting systems. After all, it's not the history that really intrigues you; intrigue is reserved for the present and the future, and quite rightly so. Thus, in most instances most of you will leave the design of the chart of accounts to a financial controller, but with the instruction that "I want to know everything important." Lumbered with this brief, and furthermore deceived by the sales talk of software vendors about the potential of accounting packages for small-to-medium businesses, the controller will use all the possibilities of the accounting software to record and view

It Couldn't Happen to You—or Could It?
TIME OUT 2.6
Customer and Sales: Who Needs Them Anyway?

I experienced the most striking example of the "hit them with the detail that can be got" but "pay no attention to the difficult stuff" phenomenon in the yearly planning cycle for a medium-sized manufacturing multinational with seven subsidiaries. My involvement started as managing director (MD) for one of the subsidiaries that had been losing money for some time.

The planning cycle consisted of the budget only. The budget started with the number of working days in each month and progressed from there to the derived number of theoretical production hours, then to the forecasted production hours and product numbers for each month via, naturally, the theoretical wastage percentages and down-time hours. From this, in almost elegant simplicity, were derived the actual sales figures that needed to be achieved in order to keep the production lines busy and the inventory at acceptable levels. Product pricing was determined by a similar exercise to arrive at the targeted and required margins.

All this data was contained in one glorious spreadsheet in which the number of linked fields, formulas, conditional statements, and related subsheets would have stretched the imagination of even a Microsoft spreadsheet designer, albeit a junior one. It was colossal! There were but a few people who could actually feed this beast and the owner-manager was not one of them.

When I asked about the sales forecasts during my first exposure to this marvel of spreadsheet brilliance, the entrepreneur said, "Sales have never been a problem. We have always managed to sell what we produce." I thought it was better not to remind him, at that first meeting anyway, that sales and pricing were the main reasons that losses had been incurred for some time.

expenditures in three, sometimes even four or more dimensions—from left to right, above and below, sideways on, and, naturally, combinations of the various categories, made possible through that marvel of the modern system, the report writer. Unfortunately, but too late, it will be realized that all these categories need to be filled by data via some sort of coding system. And unfortunately yet again no one, bar the accounting staff, has the time or the inclination, or for that matter the urge, to correctly code all invoices and expenses. Therefore, coding is done exclusively by junior financial staff with scant reference to the initiator of the expense, hence severely curtailing or even deforming accuracy and reality.

Reports from this type of "too large a fit for purpose" accounting system tend to ooze detail but lack accuracy. No one really looks at it, least of all typical entrepreneurs, who will get lost in the detail. If they ask a question they get a most unsatisfactory answer, to their minds, from the accounting staff.

Operational personnel seldom have access to the system. They might get the monthly report, but it means nothing to them. After all, all that they were "guilty" of was to incur the expense! They plead ignorance and another query disappears into the memory of the relevant entrepreneur as "nobody seems to know what they are talking about." As there certainly is no direct link between the internal financial reporting, the official accounting information, and the SENIC business's bank balance, the whole exercise is dismissed by a lot of you as a waste of time. That is not far off the mark.

Most entrepreneurs I have known had photographic memories and they all had the important bits of information "on-line," that is, in their head, anyway. As management and supervision were frequently not involved in the compilation of the budget, their enthusiasm or interest in explaining deviations from the forecasts was minimal. Nevertheless, every year another budget is produced and every month the appropriate printouts, such as, expenditure against budget by month, year to date, to go, and so forth, are generated and distributed.

Oh, that Sales Forecast

Expense control and reporting are relatively straightforward exercises, so it must come as no great surprise once again to the reader that deviations from the sales figures are a real mystery chase. As frequently there is no underlying data to support the sales forecasts, that is not really a startling revelation either.

This "budget against actual" is more often than not the sum total of management information in SENIC businesses that one comes across. Particularly when it comes to sales, get behind the numbers and find out why certain trends are happening, why you are not hitting your 1 in 5 conversion rate (orders to quotes), why you missed that last contract, or why you are losing customers to a competitor. You might think that your competition cannot survive on those low price offers because after all, "You know the cost parameters." But do you really? Look at them again, practice inverse marketing, examine your production, and so forth.

Cash Flow in Disguise

Debtor and creditor control accounts are kept in better order as a rule. That is also because the auditors[13] show much more interest in these accounts than the detailed budget expense categories. Here another phenomenon rears its troublesome head. I often refer to it as the Nice Guy Syndrome. Why? Because a great number of entrepreneurs, from the ones I have known anyway, had difficulty asking for their money for services rendered or products delivered. Some clients even set their own payment schedules and were capable of making an entrepreneur, feel guilty about asking for payment. The reason why these clients stayed with the SENIC businesses in question is very simple as well. Where else could they get those favorable payment terms?

It Couldn't Happen to You—or Could It?
TIME OUT 2.7
What Are Friends For?

The setting is a small industrial kitchen fit-out and supply company with about fifty employees. "Follow on" entrepreneur, let's call him Bob, was the son of the original entrepreneur who had died a few years earlier. Bob's brother, a professional accountant, was not involved in the business but was used as an advisor.

The business had been losing money for some time when I got involved. Overdue debtors were substantial at about 30 percent of sales, with a lot of them well over the payment terms. And this was not in Southern Europe! After some investigation, most of the overdue debt related to fit-outs where some relatively minor items were not completed. For example, badly fitted skirting boards, a couple of missing tiles under the sink, handles for cupboards, and so forth.

With Bob and his brother I agreed that we would put a small team on all the outstanding work. After that, the entrepreneur, Bob, would go and "chase" the money. After a few weeks, I noticed that Bob had become very elusive and was often unavailable, saying, "No time, I have to chase the money you know." As it materialized, Bob had been going to his old cronies, the outstanding accounts, and instead of settling the account had sold them additional items, a fridge here, a microwave there, and a coffee machine everywhere.

When I asked Bob about the outstanding payments he said, "I couldn't ask. After all they are my friends, I've known them for many years, and they told me that they can't afford to pay at the moment." So Bob, the brother, and I met again. This time we agreed that I should go with Bob and put some power behind the demand for payment.

The very first client we visited was quite an experience. Bob and the client were old acquaintances, drank many cups of coffee, and talked about everything but money. When I tried to steer the conversation the money way, the client became quite indignant and told me in no uncertain terms that he and Bob had that all sorted and who was I to get involved? He also addressed Bob and said, "After all these years of doing business together, you treat me like this!"

Other Operational Systems

Production and inventory control systems are also as varied as the industries and entrepreneurs I have encountered, ranging from none at all to the most sophisticated that money could buy. Regrettably, what they all had in common was that none of these production and inventory control systems even vaguely resembled the true state of affairs. Not enough supervisory time was set aside to manage the system, and the average production operator, service engineer, or warehouse clerk had no time and no inclination "to feed the monster." After all, the chances of getting some useful information back from the monster were almost unheard of.

Sales systems tended to be of the "address and appointment diary plus comments" variety. An almost cunning direct inverse relationship between the amount of detail recorded in the system and actual sales scores was not uncommon. Perhaps energetic and successful sales people did not have the time—possibly—nor the inclination—probably—to record every happening with a client in the central system. They seemed to prefer the actual practice of selling to data recording.

ISO Systems

A special mention must still be made of the notoriously contentious ISO systems. The whole field of quality and total quality has generated a new breed of consultants, namely, those that introduce these systems into SENIC and probably entrepreneurial businesses as well. Some of these consultants even claim that they are in the *process reengineering* field. The mind boggles. If ever there was an unnecessary paper trail that contributed nothing to operating performance and excellence, for SENIC businesses anyway, then it must be the various ISO procedures. The "Manual" is often a well-copied document in which the name of the business is inserted in the appropriate fields and "the procedures" are adjusted from well-used standard ones with minor amendments to make them applicable to the particular business. The query noted in Chapter 1 by one of the entrepreneurs about ISO 9002—"Can't we just buy it?"—is not far off the mark. Yes you can, but you must engage a quality-control consultant who will buy it for you at a price.

ISO audits are a joke because only paper trails are investigated, and as long as the SENIC business employs a diligent and meticulous bureaucrat, you will pass. That includes the famous customer-satisfaction surveys. What a wonderful money-making machine for the quality-control industry. I wonder what the original quality gurus or the Japanese initiators of the total quality credo would have to say about this state of quality management? Barring state and semi-state enterprises, and some of the multinational manufacturers, who can afford the bureaucracy, not many SENIC organizations have reaped real quality benefits from the introduction of these elaborate paper trails.

Nevertheless, you, the entrepreneur should be happy. You can display your ISO symbol(s) and the world knows that you have also passed the standard(s). (Yes, I understand that some businesses must obtain ISO certification to do business in certain industries or with certain partners. But I just had to vent.)

Health-and-Safety Requirements

Health-and-safety regulations are a completely different kettle of fish. Unfortunately, often the same quality-management consultants are involved because, as one of them put it to me, "The documentation [quality control and health-and-safety] fits elegantly together." Regrettably for the entrepreneur, there is more paper work and, in this case, ultimate and real responsibility. Here the biggest difficulty I have encountered is the absence of the "lead by example" mentality. Now I know that you, the current entrepreneur reader, would never condone behavior like this, but time and again the biggest perpetrators of basic and essential health-and-safety regulations were entrepreneurs and their inner circle employees. The good old entrepreneurial days of "let's get it done at all cost" were probably not very conducive to policies and procedures. Hence health-and-safety were not considered priorities unless real life tragedy had struck and a major incident was the result. Now that your business is aspiring to the bigger league you better get serious about health and safety.

Personnel Systems

Personnel administration systems in SENIC businesses tend to be very basic. Only the information to pay employees and to satisfy the income tax requirements is kept on file. Employment contracts are often nonexistent or consist of a note on the file. Conditions of employment, particularly with the old-timers, the inner- and outer-circle employees, are verbally agreed with the entrepreneur. The financial controller or clerk who tries to keep a record of essential salary-related information, such as overtime worked, holiday entitlement, and so forth, is fighting a losing battle. Depending on the pecking order, that is, the hierarchy, it's a relative free-for-all ball game with no rules.

A typical example was the entrepreneur of a 250-employee business. He just watched the "personnel game" and only intervened when he felt that someone did not deserve a payment, the cost of overtime got out of hand, or key employees had been away on holiday too long for his liking. His inner-circle employees didn't really go on holiday because even on holiday they phoned in every day to find out what was going on. One of these inner circle employees claimed 145 days holiday due to him. When I asked him why he had not pointed out this fact to John, the owner-manager, he said mockingly, "Point it out to John? You know that John never listens. He just keeps telling me, you must take your holidays. But you can't go now."

Market forces have dictated some sort of salary structures, but inner-circle employees tend to be rewarded according to their ability to ask for more. I have come across well-qualified engineers with ten years' faithful service who got paid less than half of what a production planner of similar vintage, but who was both politically astute but nowhere near as valuable to the business, was paid.

Don't think that the previous descriptions of systems are related only to very small SENIC businesses. The SENIC businesses I am talking about often employed a hundred people or more and had quite respectable sales. Not surprisingly, in the very small businesses, there always appeared to be unofficial systems of peer control and "human memory checks and balances" on operational systems. Overview was easier for managers who could correct data directly and quite simply. Therefore it was in the medium-sized SENIC businesses where systems were often totally out of control because peer pressure no longer worked and the multitude of tasks or activities could no longer be memorized. That's often also the time that consultants make their introduction to the SENIC scene.

Consultants

Not all consultants are bad, but it is important to realize that, when all is said and done, the purpose of the consultancy firm is no different from any other company. They supply a commercial service. They are a supplier and accordingly they want to make money. Remember the issues discussed under the "Inverse Marketing" heading in Section "Your Customers Are the Key to Growth." Treat them like suppliers and nail them down as to what it is that they are going to do. If you don't really know what it is that you want from them, leave them alone until such time that you have a properly defined project. Always keep that in the back of your mind when you hear the wonderful stories of how they can help you introduce a new system, determine your strategy, and so forth. An open-ended assignment to a consultant is like an invitation to print some money at your expense.

Most consultants[14] are not great implementers; they will cast their eye over the SENIC business in question, write their reports, make their recommendations, and collect their fees. It's you, the entrepreneur that will be left with the idea that you have not really understood their "magic" and you failed to implement some of the recommendations made in their report. Hence the result was not what you had wished for and they had promised before you signed on the dotted line. The fault is entirely yours, and yours alone. That's what they will make you believe anyway! They won't say this as directly as I have written it here, but they will remind you of their excellent standing and reputation. Thus, when you do involve consultants, take note of the points made in Appendix B.

Golden Rules for Systems

All the examples quoted previously bring us to what actually needs to be enhanced and why. Systems need to support your business functions and not hamper them. The example of the budget is a classic. From a management tool it can be turned into an obstacle by concentrating on great insignificant detail. A simple cash-flow system can be very effective, but turn it into some monster spreadsheet and it becomes a chore that requires too much effort to keep up to date on a regular basis. Try and apply the 80/20 rule to your systems. Concentrate on the Critical Success Factors, particularly during difficult times, by monitoring those critical factors closely. Often you don't need a sophisticated system to tell you that these factors are out of line. If information is sufficient or half-automated at the moment, don't try and start a major upgrade during SENIC times. Get past SENIC first. A system, automated or not, that is not delivering the "goods" will not be enhanced by the introduction of new software. Find out what makes a mockery of the existing system and fix it, amend it, or discard it. For example, no amount of sophisticated software will get you over the hurdle of making sure your debtors pay on time. A persistent and determined credit control clerk, backed up by you, will do wonders for your cash flow. Also, a new sophisticated inventory control system will not work if you have not instilled the discipline of allocating sensible stock numbers to all your stock or the inventory people work the system after the day is done because working with the system during an actual transaction is too complex or time consuming. Similarly, if your sales people fill in all the required fields during a sales visit but fail to score consistently, you better find out what is wrong. The chances are that the real reasons are not recorded, but if you would ask them straight out they might tell you. Thus remember that SENIC, first and foremost, is about "people systems" and not about "systems systems."

FOULS
- Permitting a too-complex budget.
- Developing one-liner sales forecasts.
- Not involving sales personnel in collecting overdue accounts.
- Letting feeding the operating system become a chore, rather than an integrated task. It's one-way traffic.
- Making quality and health-and-safety programs merely paper trails.
- Permitting lack of detail in personnel files.
- Letting numerous consultants "pass through."

FREE THROWS
- Concentrate on CSFs (Critical Success Factors) in your system(s).
- Fix it before you computerize it.
- Remember: The system is only as good as the people who maintain it.
- Let systems support you, not strangle you.
- Dig for the Truth. Good systems don't tell lies, but don't necessarily tell the truth either.

SOME FORMALITIES AND RULES ARE REQUIRED

The conventional definition of management is getting work done through people, but real management is developing people through work.

Agha Hasan Abedi (1922–1995)

Delegation Is the Art

There are two management principles that really must be implemented during the SENIC phase in order "to overcome and conquer," and those are the principles of authority and responsibility. They must be developed in tandem because authority without responsibility leads to a "why should I care?" attitude, and responsibility without authority leads to an "I care but why?" approach. These two principles are the basis of a sound system of delegation. The art of delegation requires a lot more than giving people things to do and letting them get on with it. It requires regular reporting, frequent feedback and corrections agreed by both the employee and the superior to retain effectiveness in executing the various business tasks. Thus a prerequisite for successful delegation is that logical grouped business tasks are allocated to particular functions. Thus the time has arrived that you, the entrepreneur, define your organization, name the functions, and allocate responsibilities, coupled to authorities naturally, to these functions. It's almost imperative that this formal exercise is carried out at the SENIC stage in order to lighten your own load, to see what some of your senior people are really capable of, and to address gaps in your organization.

It requires a bit of thought to divide all tasks into manageable chunks, that is, management jobs that are logical in terms of your business, and what's more, define these jobs in terms of their purpose and objectives. This exercise is best achieved without thinking of the people that you currently employ. Just think of the tasks that need to be done in order to make the business run effectively. If at all possible compose job descriptions[15] for your major functions and only then try and fit people to the jobs. That's why implementation is so difficult. You, the entrepreneur, needs to think of the tasks that need to be achieved and then allocate them to the most suitable persons in your current organization—not easy, but vital, if SENIC is to be conquered!

In a sense you are saying goodbye to the informal creative days of the past and welcoming the more structured approach that must carry you through SENIC and onwards to greater size in turnover, staffing, and income. Your first official management team has now become reality.

Implementation Is the Science

The practice of defining the organization with some one-page job descriptions is not a complex one, but as usual the difficulty lies in the implementation and not the definition. The implementation requires that

It Couldn't Happen to You—or Could It?
TIME OUT 2.8
Consistency: Easy to Preach Difficult to Practice

The plan was made, the organization had been defined, and the new management team was being kick started with a well-planned meeting. The entrepreneur, let's call him Edward, was dead keen to share some responsibilities with his team. He and a good business friend, whom he trusted explicitly, had selected the team a few weeks earlier on the basis of seniority and dedication to the business. Edward had started this particular manufacturing business some eight years ago and had gone from strength to strength. However, of late with the latest big order "safely in the bag" things started to go wrong. Delivery times were not met, production was working 14 hours a day, six days a week, complaints about bad quality had increased, and some older customers were decidedly unhappy. The cash flow came under considerable pressure due to increases in raw material purchases and considerable overtime payments. To put not too fine a point to it, Edward's business was well into SENIC.

The first management meeting was convened; Edward took the chair and worked through the agenda with efficiency and speed. Afterwards he did admit that his team had been a bit silent, but nevertheless he felt good about the whole thing. After all, it was the first time they met as a group. Most contacts to date had been on a face-to-face basis with a "can do" attitude. When asked, every one present admitted that it had been a good session. No one was asked to compile action points or minutes. Next week, same time, same place, was the enthusiastic slogan.

Next week came around. Unfortunately there had been no time to prepare an agenda but nevertheless the meeting was held. After all, they all knew what the real problems were. The meeting lasted for the better part of a day, but Edward started to realize that most of the talking had been done by him. In hindsight Edward even had the uncomfortable feeling that nothing much was achieved, but these were still early days. Thus Edward decided to press on regardless. After all, consistency was important! After a few more weeks, what had now turned into a one-man show was getting on Edward's "you know what" and into his head as well. His team did not seem to understand the urgency of the situation and he felt that he was still carrying the full load of responsibility. Plenty of problems but no solutions! He was getting more and more agitated at the weekly meetings, his lengthy orations appeared to fall on deaf ears, and what good were these meetings anyway? They had achieved a hell of a lot without these long sessions. Nevertheless Edward decided to press on and keep at it. He decided each week what had to be discussed; after all it was his business! As time passed, the new management team started to avoid his eyes during his lengthy and sometimes aggressive orations. He seldom addressed a team member by name, but appeared to chastise them all in turn in front of each other.

A few weeks later Edward could not make the meeting. He was at a potential new client and could not get away in time. He asked Peter, the production manager and his right hand man from the early pioneering days, to lead the meeting and report back to him afterwards. When he did get back to the office the next day, he clean forgot about the meeting and Peter never volunteered any information either. The following week, Edward forgot the meeting, no one reminded him either, and the week after, Edward had no time to even think about meetings. He told Peter to run the meetings in his absence. Peter tried for a few weeks but Edward "the force" was missing and the meetings degenerated into "comfortable breaks from real work," as one of the team members expressed it. Edward never mentioned team or meeting again.

you, the entrepreneur, delegate most of the day-to-day tasks to your new management team. The key word of course is *delegate*. Read the previous paragraph again and keep on reminding yourself what *delegation* means. Make time available for regular one-on-one and management meetings. *Regularity* is the key word here. In the beginning it is important to have frequent but short meetings to make sure that you and your team are all playing football on the same pitch and there aren't a couple of rugby players that are hell bent on playing their own game.

Don't compile minutes of meetings. In my experience minutes are not about what people actually said but what people would have liked to have said after they have seen the minutes, or even worse, recalled what they should have said if there had been no minutes. It's much more effective for a small management team to keep a list of action points; each one of these should be the responsibility of a member of the team with the due date for completion. Action points should be very specific, such as, evaluate suppliers for raw material X as to price, delivery, and quality by the end of next month. They should also be related to a Critical Success Factor (CSF).

When you feel that your message is getting across make sure that you are getting more and more input from your team. Now here comes another difficult part.

Active Listening

Most entrepreneurs that I have known are very good and forceful in making their point but are poor listeners. If you want power sharing and feedback, let your team develop the skill of presenting their ideas while you practice the art of active listening or "counting to ten" as I often call it. Every time you feel like interrupting someone, count to ten, in slow motion please, before you actually do. It's their confidence that needs building not yours. You have enough of it, believe me! They need to acquire the art of disagreeing with you without having their heads bitten off. Compliance is not good enough any more; you need to be challenged from time to time. They might not be right but with you listening, and the others making the points, you are developing into a real team. The team must be greater than each individual member. With your business development skills and their newly acquired management skills you have laid the foundation for *post SENIC*.

Supervisory Skills

Perhaps, it's also time to send your chosen management team to a supervisory course. It is imperative that they should attend as a team and that the course is run specifically for your team. Apart from teaching them the basics of supervising personnel, including managing their own work, it will strengthen their feeling that the team is greater than each individual member. There are plenty of good supervisory training courses around. After the course is finished, make sure you get feedback from each one of your managers and from the course leader. After all, you are still in charge and need to know what has been learned and where the weaknesses are. Challenge the course leader to give you feedback on each individual manager. His opinion might point to strengths and weaknesses in each one of the managers. It's always possible that one of them is not quite up to the task, but having selected them, you must give them a chance. Also, let them manage their respective teams and accept that there are many ways to skin a cat and your way is not necessarily the best for any given situation. It's the result that counts—not the way the result is achieved as long as it's legal and of benefit to your business.

Trial-and-Error and Focus

It is not uncommon for entrepreneurs to grab the nearest employee and let him do something that needs to be done immediately. It has worked in the past under the "we are all in this together" mentality. Now that the organization is a bit larger, and in SENIC, don't forget this mentality will probably lead to a considerable amount of confusion and sometimes even abdication by the person who should have been responsible. After you have officially defined the organization and appointed your management team, you will have to find the manager that you have made responsible for the particular activity and let him get on with it. It sounds easy but will take some time before it starts to work properly.

Herald the trial-and-error phase! There probably are some grey areas that are unclear as to who does what in particular situations. These are problems that need to be resolved if and when they occur. If they are fundamental, discuss with your management team, adjust the relevant job descriptions, and try again. If they are not, remind employees that job descriptions are guidelines only and need to be interpreted with a spirit of cooperation in mind. You don't want to achieve a situation where employees hide behind the job description or, even worse, "work to rule." You also don't want to be left with grey areas where things happen that have always happened but nobody really knew why they happened. All employees should "belong" to one of your managers. You must get used to operating your organization with your managers and not bypass them.

In the past I have come across the weirdest situations. For example, in one case, the supervisor of a depot was located some twenty miles from the main factory. The location was almost a little business on its own. The supervisor was buying and selling to his heart's delight based on the simple fact that the entrepreneur had once told him to just "get rid of those spare items" at the best possible price. And then there were the employees that did "specific" non-business-related things for the entrepreneur in a workshop environment. They were a law unto themselves, and kept the rest of the organization wondering why they could "claim" a production lathe for a couple of hours, always seemed to be on a smoking break, and the safety regulations did not appear to apply to them. I have known an entrepreneur with a SENIC but basically sound manufacturing business that also had a shop, two bars, and a couple of rent-a-trucks in the nearby town. Guess who was called frequently to repair things in these unrelated activities? Suddenly production targets in the main business didn't seem to matter. It was almost like his hobby was found in the unrelated bits or was perhaps a form of diversification.

These types of anomalies must be eliminated in order to get everyone focused in on the job at hand, namely the survival of the business. If as an entrepreneur you do have some other activities, don't mix them with your main business, namely, the one we are discussing now. Survival is at stake, and diversions of the kind just described will take your own eye but also your team's eye off the ball until you lose the ball altogether. Don't give anyone excuses for deviations. Focus is crucial during tough times. Focus the management team and yourself on the Critical Success Factors (CSFs) of the main SENIC business.

Operational Policies or Rules

With delegation also comes the time for laying down some operational rules. For example, what is the credit policy of your company? You cannot expect the credit-control person to effectively implement a policy when the rules are being stretched by every client who claims your acceptance to his personal conditions. Also, it is no good to provide pricing guidelines to your salespeople and then override them if clients phone you direct. Don't hold the production manager to task on production schedules when you interfere continually to satisfy demands from some old clients who phone you in their quest to achieve preference. What exactly is your delivery time promise to your major clients? What is your "Goods Return Policy" like? No doubt you are getting the message. So if you do decide on some policies and procedures, stick with them personally as well. That's probably more difficult for you than your employees, but you will have to live by your own rules if you want to be taken seriously by all, and in particular by your management team.

SENIC can be conquered if you delegate properly and realize that the good old days are over and order needs to prevail. What's even more important is that the burden of making the business move forward has to be shared by its senior employees. And sharing responsibility is achieved at its best if there are some basic policies and rules that everyone adheres to. At the end of the day rules and policies are there for making sure that your organization presents itself with a single face to the market place. Flexibility is nice, but ultimate flexibility is chaos and that's not the sort of chaos Tom Peters (1988)[16] advocates.

Staff Policies

SENIC time is also the right time to think about introducing some formal personnel (or if you like, human resources) policies. Think in particular about working hours, working practices, overtime rates, facilities, benefits, and so forth. Ask for input from employees and discuss every serious suggestion. If someone felt strong enough to bring it up, it should at least be discussed and evaluated as to its practicability.

Have a good look at your remuneration policy, get some information on market rates in your industry, and get the "bones" in place for some sort of salary structure or "pecking order" if you like. That's important because comparisons are made all the time. Most employees are well aware of what others in the same organization earn. Salaries have always been the most public secret in any company that I have ever worked for. Take it from me, ninety-five percent of your employees know what every one else is earning. They make it their mission to find out. In smaller companies, the wages clerks sitting on this potential valuable source of information are only human. They part with it quite easily because it's "oh so nice" to have confidential information that everyone wants to get hold of. Thus, the more equitable your system of remuneration, the more "rest" is created in the organization. If you want to be creative in rewarding your employees by means of stock options, bonuses, and so forth, make sure you first work out what it is going to cost you. SENIC is not the best time to realize at year's end that you owe your employees large sums of money in bonuses. Salespeople are, particularly, masters at manipulating bonus schemes to their advantage by employing every loophole possible. It's similar to tax avoidance; every time the government closes a loophole the astute tax advisors make or discover a leak somewhere else. So don't get involved in complex remuneration schemes; just concentrate on getting over SENIC and rewarding employees fairly.

FOULS
- Assigning responsibility divorced from authority.
- Overpowering your team.
- Bypassing your team.

- Getting diverted by extracurricular activities.
- Breaking your own rules.
- Creating ad-hoc remuneration systems.

FREE THROWS
- Remember: Delegation is the art.
- Implementation is the science.
- Develop the art of active listening.
- Send your management team to a supervisory skills course.
- Employ trial and error: Nothing is written in stone.
- Focus, focus, and focus again.
- Develop a single "face" for your company.

NOTES

1. Special Report, "The World's Oldest Companies," *The Economist* (December 18, 2004): 3.

2. Ranft, A. L. and O'Neill, H. M., "The Perils of Power," *Sloan Management Review*, Vol. 43, Number 3, p. 13.

3. It is absolutely amazing what can be learned from the employees who do the actual work. In my experience, some of the most effective suggestions for improvements in all spheres of operational activities have always come from what is often referred to as "the floor."

4. Hamel, Gary, "Killer Strategies," *Fortune* 35 (June 23, 1997): 70.

5. Mintzberg, Henry, *The Rise and Fall of Strategic Planning* (Englewood Cliffs, NJ: Prentice Hall, 1994), 284).

6. Bennis, W. and Nanus, B., *Leaders: The Strategies for Taking Charge* (New York: Harper & Row, 1985).

7. Henry Mintzberg, Bruce Ahlstrand, and Joseph Lampel, *Strategy Safari* (New York: Free Press, 1998), 137.

8. If you are in a position to determine "contribution to overhead" for each account, so much the better.

9. It does not help that the neighbors of a typical inner-circle employee always seem to work for what others would call "that reputable, large, ever-so-good-to-their-people, why-can't-you-get-a-job-there," business. The neighbor always leaves at nine and returns, without fail, at four, still has fifteen days holiday left and never works on Saturdays and Sundays. Oh, the pain!

10. "A Small Business Is Not a Little Big Business," *Harvard Business Review*, 59 (July 1, 1981): 18–32.

11. The term *controller* is used loosely to describe the person who keeps the accounts in a SENIC business, not necessarily a qualified accountant.

12. Why this was not done was most eloquently explained to me, in this case anyway, by a controller for a SENIC business with 150 employees, as follows: "They [the other members of the management team] don't understand it. After

all it's only me who has to explain to Tony [the owner-manager] why costs are out of hand; no one else has ever been held to task."

13. Don't we just love auditors? The way the partner of the audit firm comes and starts off the process followed by the introduction of one or more juniors who have to be spoon-fed for the next fourteen days as to where the information can be found! In particular, stock takes and determining stock value can be great fun!

14. Unfortunately most management consultants are expert theoreticians who never in their life had the responsibility of executing their suggested strategies and plans. Even McKinsey, that Don of the Management Consulting Industry admitted that, "Making real decisions in a business is a lot harder than getting paid to advise people what to do" (O'Shea and Madigan, 1999; see bibliography).

15. A simple format for job descriptions, consisting of purpose of the job, main tasks, and objectives for the current year will do. Some examples are given as Appendix 7.4.

16. Peters, Tom, *Thriving on Chaos: Handbook for a Management Revolution* (New York: Harper Paperbacks, 1988).

3

Common Failures of Post-entrepreneurial Businesses

It is not enough to do your best; you must know what to do, and then do your best.

W. Edwards Deming (1900–1993)

INTRODUCTION

Many a man's reputation would not know his character if they met on the street.

Elbert Hubbard (1856–1915)

This chapter is not easy reading for you, the champion of the start-up business, the entrepreneur admired by family, friends, and employees. And that's not because it's difficult to read but because almost all of you don't like to be reminded that failure is still an option. Yes, your first organizational crisis might mean that your business fails. Yes, I mean Fail[1] with a capital F! After all, the survival rates of post-entrepreneurial businesses are far from encouraging, and you won't hear me argue about these statistics. So why should you be able to beat the odds?

As can be expected, success makes better reading than failure, but for the moment you have to forget the best sellers with remarkable success stories for a while. That type of star performance is very rare indeed, and what's even more to the point, virtually impossible to copy. Failure, on the contrary, is much more commonplace, and does it not stand to reason, therefore, that one can learn more from failure than from success? If you approach this chapter with the outlook of someone who wants to learn from past failures and recognize, or perhaps even relate your own circumstances to some of the symptoms that led to failure, you are way ahead of the game and ready for the hard decisions that have to be made. The move beyond SENIC can be launched when you have diagnosed your own situation honestly, openly, and correctly.

This then is the purpose of this chapter: to help you recognize the symptoms so you can start concentrating on the cure.

At the SENIC Center: You and You Alone

The responsibility for the current crisis of leadership, the SENIC phase (Still Evolving, Now in Crisis), lies primarily with you, the entrepreneur—after all, you are the business. There's no doubt about that at all. So take the responsibility. Convince yourself that the solution lies primarily with you and you alone as well. For the time being, forget the past successes and adapt. That's the key to continuance in a single word: *adapt.* Yesterday is gone, tomorrow is waiting with new challenges, different certainly but just as exciting as the ones conquered before. Your business has grown and you must grow with it. If you don't like it, then get out of this particular business game. In business school jargon, design an exit strategy, or, if you prefer, ask for your ball back and tell everyone you don't want to play anymore.

Without you adapting to the new challenge of getting beyond SENIC how do you expect your employees to adapt? At the SENIC stage, leadership and management are required more than anything else to make change possible. You probably are a leader all right, but are you a manager too? Just to know what you want to change and doing it are no longer enough. You need to do it in the "management sense" to surmount the current crisis.

So there is quite a lot of personal stuff in this chapter, with discussions on: differences between management and entrepreneurship, setting examples, getting out of the "fire brigade," and so forth.

Staff and Family: Your Responsibility Too

It's time again to do some soul searching about whether your staff is really suitable for the task at hand. Remember, they are the DNA of your company and their capabilities are directly related to your future success. The "fun to have around" factor needs to be examined in view of the "fit for purpose" capability.

What's also introduced in this chapter is the burden that your family can start to exert on your business if you let its influence go unchecked. There is nothing wrong with employing members of your extended family, but are they fit for the purpose? Family members or other political appointments might satisfy your relatives or your ego, but are they good for the business? Besides, if these appointments are not really adding value to your business, your regular employees will scarcely be motivated by such actions.

SENIC is real serious stuff as you must realize by now, and diversions created by wrong appointments or family favors will not help you at all. Refer to some of the family-related experiences and make sure they will never happen on your watch!

Customers and Cash Flow

Cash flow and customers are two reliable contributors to many a business failure during SENIC phase. From the latter there might be too many, there might not be enough, or there is too much "variety." All three of these positions can lead to serious difficulties in cash flow because it's the

It Couldn't Happen to You—or Could It?
TIME OUT 3.1
It's Not What You Know but Who You Know

A food-manufacturing company employed about 150 employees in the early 1990s. The company had been losing money for the last couple of years—not a desperate situation, but bad enough. The main problem was consistency and quality in production and hence a fair number of dissatisfied customers.

Entrepreneur-in-Crisis has had enough, and wants to pull out. He has employed me to reorganize and get profitability back before he attempts a sale of the business. Entrepreneur has one child, a daughter, the apple of his eye, who thus far has shown no interest in the business at all. There is a vacancy on the production floor for a supervisor. It's a critical appointment; this is where the problems are. There are two internal candidates, both equally suitable, both of them with about ten years of faithful and loyal service. Tough decision! I try to be polite and ask my entrepreneur for his opinion. He behaves evasively, changes the subject, and says we will discuss it next week. I think this is strange, as the appointment is rather urgent.

Next week rolls around. Entrepreneur calls me and announces, "I have a candidate for the job, a good eager fellow, interviewed him last week and he is starting tomorrow." I'm flabbergasted. Both internal candidates are totally de-motivated and disgusted, to put it mildly. The story spreads like wildfire, real tabloid stuff. Everyone forgets work for quite a while. Above all, my authority is shot to hell!

What happened? It's a girl meets boy story. His daughter had fallen madly in love with this fellow, let's call him Romeo, who was looking for a job. No qualifications, some experience as an office clerk, but other more passionate virtues no doubt. Daughter did the "Daddy, please, pretty please," bit, and what can you do?

incoming, or lack of incoming, cash that often creates the problem. The expense side is far easier to control. Thus customers and cash flow also occupy a well-deserved place in this chapter on why post-entrepreneurial businesses fail.

FREE THROWS
- Take responsibility for company crises.
- Ask: Are family members up to the task of helping the company grow?
- Never forget: Cash flow is king.

MANAGEMENT AND ENTREPRENEURSHIP:
OFTEN THE TWAIN DON'T MIX

> When I attack entrepreneurs, I quote managers. And When I attack managers, I quote entrepreneurs.
>
> The Writer

The predominant (and may I add successful) management style during the entrepreneurial phase (typified by creation and informality) is regrettably also the cause of the first big organizational problem, that is, SENIC. Thus what comes naturally in the start-up years has to be modified to become a more structured approach in running your current business. This means that you, the entrepreneur, needs to learn how to acquire most of the skills of a general manager. So how difficult is this adaptation? To find out, let's compare the behavioral characteristics of entrepreneurs with those of general managers. Comparing entrepreneurial styles with management styles leads to some striking differences.

Entrepreneurial vs. Management Style

Entrepreneurs tend to be action and expression oriented, whereas managers prefer analysis and harmony. While the entrepreneur is inventive, productive, and acts swiftly to gain advantage, the manager acts more cautiously, prefers to analyze systems critically, and disperses information efficiently. Entrepreneurs seek immediate results but managers seek predictability and continuity. Entrepreneurs are idea people, creators, conceptualizers, and front enders. They don't usually enjoy the details of implementation. Early success can lead to failure when they have to compromise their natural talents of creating business opportunities in favor of managing their own ventures. Hence the two concepts of creating and destroying are often separated only by a thin dividing line.

In contrast, managers can bog down in the detail and lose a lot of time in the process. They can be overly sensitive to feedback and might even appear to lack courage. Managers can be warm and supportive of others, relatively easy going and relaxed, and reliable and consistent. Entrepreneurs are forceful and impatient, often think their own way is best, can be insensitive to others, and tend to be manipulative. One could go on like this for quite some time and come to the conclusion that the entrepreneurial style and the managerial style are mutually exclusive.

These two styles are so different that the typical entrepreneur can never convert to a typical general manager. That is ever so true—but, fortunately, typical profiles are seldom encountered in real life. Hence there is a better-than-average chance of success!

Entrepreneur Know Thyself

Let's call a typical entrepreneur a 100/0 and a typical manager a 0/100. The chances of success for yourself the entrepreneur during the SENIC phase are probably best if you are a 50/50. While 50 percent of you got the venture off the ground, the other 50 percent of you made all the right management decisions to overcome the organizational crisis as a matter of course. Just a walk in the park!

Unfortunately, 50/50s are probably just as rare as 100/0 and 0/100s. So the odds are that your own character profile is either biased towards the entrepreneurial side or towards the management side. For the former group I would pose the question very delicately, "Are you really sure you want to go it alone?" Consider very carefully. You might not like the idea of bringing in an outsider to help run your business. But what is more important, your personal feelings or the development of the business? Think about it!

To the latter group of potential Do It Yourself crisis beaters I would say, "If managing is what you really want to do, go for it!" Test yourself on how you have shaped up so far as a general manager. Here is one of the best tests for this: Do you allow your employees to disagree with you and do you respect their opinions? If the answer is "no," watch out.

Also you must like managing. Nothing is more miserable than being involved in organization-building while all you really want to do is develop the next bright idea. Think about it sensibly and then decide. You can always get temporary but full-time assistance if you need it, and outside help for specific, well-defined projects.

Adapt

Unfortunately a lot of entrepreneurs do not realize that a business at SENIC does need firm direction much more than informality and creativity. Hence a lot of failures are due to the lack of management skills of the entrepreneur. That's why the message is so important. Recognize the symptoms, take action and survive, or ignore them at your peril. Now quite a few of you might say, "Creativity is the essence of growth." That's also true, but NOT during SENIC. The firm foundation for a sound business must be laid during this turbulent period in order to cope with future growth. Future growth can be stimulated by continuous improvement and creativity, but only after consolidation has been achieved.

What's in Store

The next section is perhaps a look ahead for you, the new post-entrepreneurial business owner, but not that far in the future either. It relates very much to my experiences with businesses and in particular entrepreneurs who did not realize the consequences of the transformation from entrepreneurial to directional (more professional, dispassionate management). The longer you leave the crisis to itself, the more difficult it becomes to take the appropriate action. So if you like, look at the next section as an eye opener as to what lies in store if no action is taken when SENIC is reached. Read some of the symptoms that I have encountered over the last twenty odd years or so and then do some soul searching. Put more bluntly, entrepreneur: know your own strengths and weaknesses.

FOULS
- Not facing up to SENIC requirements.
- Not knowing the difference in management styles from entrepreneurial to directional.
- Being a 100/0 and not admitting it!

FREE THROWS
- For those of you that are in the 80 to 100/0 ball park on the entrepreneurial-to-management scale, get yourself a general manager!

KNOW YOUR OWN STRENGTHS (AND WEAKNESSES)

Whenever I climb I am followed by a dog called "ego."
Friedrich Nietzsche (1844–1900)

This section is written in a more impersonal form to illustrate what could happen if you don't take action. You, the entrepreneur, might think it's all a bit over the top, but at least appreciate the fact that an outsider has taken the trouble to describe the various SENIC scenarios from his own experiences. It might just make you appreciate your own strengths and weaknesses and spur you into action. Because what is described could be the "vision turned nightmare" if you don't take action during the early stages of SENIC. Your greatest strength might turn into a formidable weakness that'll wear you down relentlessly.

Attribution Bias

Entrepreneurs are the life and soul of SENIC businesses. Within the organization there almost certainly will be a management structure in place and there might even be some semblance of decision-making ability in the ranks. There might even be some small family shareholdings or an insignificant stake that in a weak moment[2] was given to some of the senior employees.

But let's not fool ourselves. There is only one person who holds all of the reins, whether we are talking about buying stationery or closing the next major deal. The entrepreneur is the person in charge, the real driving and deciding force of the SENIC business without any doubt whatsoever. Driven by hard work and a need to achieve, entrepreneurs have established their own barriers, have a strong need to take charge of situations, and have to be in control. Entrepreneurs are self-starters who need no encouragement from others, thrive on extreme pressure and deadlines, and believe that it is generally easier to do things themselves than to show others how to do them.

A fair number of entrepreneurs in my experience—present company excepted, of course—show signs of *attribution bias*,[3] not unlike the corporate fat cats of the many twentieth-century boom periods.

But ironically, entrepreneurs also need to be overconfident because they, after all, must take the personal risks that will move their businesses forward. This is in sharp contrast with the corporate fat cats whose personal risks appear to be designed along the lines of "heads you win, tails you don't lose," in terms of monetary rewards anyway.

Entrepreneur Beware!

Entrepreneurs are singularly convinced of their predetermined destiny. They have the attitude that they can succeed at just about anything. But then, sometimes bit by bit, sometimes swiftly, but always relentlessly, they are confronted with the first organizational crisis. Now, nearly all entrepreneurs are more than capable of facing any number of daunting tasks. But sadly, organizational ability is not often part of the skill set. For people who have always been in complete control and who have solved many predicaments in their early entrepreneurial days, this comes as a serious shock. As a consequence, the feeling of losing control is tremendously disconcerting even to the most confident of entrepreneurs. The business appears to be taking control of them! That's the typical feeling that any manager, entrepreneur or not, would experience during an organizational crisis.

The Elasticity Syndrome

The arrival of the crisis clearly highlights a noticeable difference in the conduct of entrepreneurs that appears to be related to their degree of actual involvement in the business. These involvement distinctions can, to my mind, be ascribed not so much to deviations of entrepreneurial character traits but more to traits that could be related to a phenomena that I am going to refer to as the "to let go or not to let go" elasticity syndrome.

In a pragmatic sense, entrepreneurs-in-crisis can be broadly graded into three distinct categories: H-ACTIVE, ACTIVE, and N-ACTIVE.

H-ACTIVE

The entrepreneurs that are still actively involved in their SENIC businesses. In the context of this book, actively means being there each and every day. At the coal mine, so to speak, with boots and all. Type: Hyperactive, or H-ACTIVE for short.

ACTIVE

The entrepreneurs who are still at the business frequently but have started another venture or ventures and have left the original business a bit to its own resources. Sometimes they have started to mention to everyone who cares to listen that they are pulling out, ready to hand over to the next generation, if there is one, or seeking some other type of continuity for their first life's work. Type: ACTIVE.

N-ACTIVE

Entrepreneurs that are no longer there but tend to interfere at will and decide almost at random. The power in absentia, so to speak. It is somewhat unclear who actually is in charge on a day-to-day basis at the SENIC organizations that they should be running. Some "employees of the first hour" act from time to time as if they are, but nobody takes that seriously. The business is a bit in limbo, but somehow enough money is made to satisfy the entrepreneur's personal demands. The entrepreneur is not really interested in another venture but is "milking" the present one. This is not very common but it does happen. Type: Not Really Active or N-ACTIVE for short.

These three categories tend to be a regressive sequence of decline, according to the "let go or not to let go" elasticity syndrome. Not all entrepreneurs go through each subsequent phase. Some stick with the first phase, H-ACTIVE, and find a solution to continue or not to continue. Some eventually get out elegantly or not so elegantly at phase ACTIVE. And some entrepreneurs—not too many, fortunately—stick with the program, yet cannot make up their mind what they really want and, by default, fall, literally and figuratively, into the last category, N-ACTIVE. Let us look at each type in a bit more detail.

H-ACTIVE

The entrepreneurs that represent this category are far in the majority. Their involvement and commitment are beyond question and they still hold all the reins. There is absolutely no doubt about that. They have their eyes continually and almost zealously on the ball. Based on my personal observations, the only thing that seems to distract some of them badly are serious disagreements in their direct family. Even this very committed type of entrepreneur can become obsessed with first sorting out the family plight and often forgets to run the business.

H-ACTIVE entrepreneurs make all the important decisions, which, in their view, they all are. They know all there is to know about their customers, their products, and their own organizations. The business is their life and hobby and they expect their employees to feel and behave in the same way. They think they are always right, decide fast, often on "gut feel," and seldom listen to advice. In many ways this is still the most successful form of entrepreneurship because they are without a doubt 100 percent committed, involved, and responsible. There is nothing wrong with that as long as all goes according to plan.

In essence, H-ACTIVE are still "the real entrepreneurs." They are the archetype autocrat, proactive, single-minded leaders who want to build a

It Couldn't Happen to You—or Could It?
TIME OUT 3.2
Mirror, Mirror on the Wall, When Can We Have an
Improvement at All?

This particular case refers to an entrepreneur, type N-ACTIVE, who had built quite a successful manufacturing business spread over a number of plants in Northern Europe. The product was of the commodity kind and could not really be altered without significant capital expenditure.

Unfortunately, the last major capital project, a more than doubling of an existing plant's capacity, was ill advised and badly executed due to his incessant and continuous interference. His own engineering staff had tried to tell him, in a weak moment no doubt, that the new addition to the plant would never work because of space restrictions and some owner-designed, far-too-complicated machinery interfaces. Designing equipment interfaces was one of his hobbies. Naturally, the engineers were told that "nothing was impossible"; all they had to do was listen to his master's voice.

Regrettably on this occasion, his engineers were right, and from the first day of operation it became quite clear that optimum capacity, due to inflexibility and poor layout, would never be reached. Also, it became clear that there was not enough demand for the product with the increased capacity and that the whole extension might have been a "bridge too far."

Over the next couple of years, salespeople pleaded, engineers tinkered, accountants analyzed, managers threatened, skilled machine operators came and went, but the problems did not recede.

When my period in office started, the plant had been operated at a substantial loss for over five years. After a few months, having had discussions with head office engineers and the local management, I had worked out a number of options in order of "time to recovery," meaning back to profitability. Some of these options involved adding value to the product by injecting more capital, but the most logical option, to me at least, was to close the extension of the plant and revert back to the original operation. This would have almost guaranteed a return to profitability in a relatively short time—my guess was about six months, albeit at the old level of production.

After a return to profitability other options requiring additional capital expenditure could be investigated. Mr. N-ACTIVE was somewhere on the seven seas so in order to prepare for this action I met with a number of financial institutions to seek additional financing for the proposed reorganization. One of these came forward with a package that incorporated the subsidiary's existing debt and shaved about 15 percent of the monthly interest costs. For me this really was the icing on the cake. When Mr. N-ACTIVE became available, I sought an audience to present him with the various options, concentrating on the preferred option and naturally the new financial package.

(Continued)

> *Tried* was the operative word here, because my presentation took all of 30 seconds. Mr. N-ACTIVE did not want to discuss any options and with a voice laden with emotion almost cried to me, "I have never failed, so I am certainly not going to fail now. The plant stays as is and you were taken on to make it profitable. So make it profitable." When I explained to him that for the last five years his staff had tried to make the additional operation profitable and had not succeeded, so maybe a different plan was ..., he interrupted me with scorn and said, "And you have been at it for three months already and there is still no sign of improvement."

strong enterprise and by and large do not allow anyone or anything to stand in their way or delay them. An extreme case of an H-ACTIVE owner-manager that I came across some years back demanded loyalty in no uncertain terms from all his employees. They had to be at his beck and call twenty-four hours a day and that was a commitment often required. When queried about anything, he used to say, "Who's paying the wages around here?"

The dominant goal of type H-ACTIVE is growth. Growth itself is often achieved by dramatic leaps forward. This works as long as the business is relatively simple and focused enough to be comprehended in one head. That is also why entrepreneurship is at the center of the most celebrated corporate successes. When it works and the circumstances are right, it can be glorious indeed. By the very nature of its exclusivity, it is a very complex act to follow for anyone, due to the inherent difficulty in predicting the next move and the unrivalled energy of the H-ACTIVE entrepreneur.

But like all good things, there is a downside. If the tide, for whatever reason, turns against H-ACTIVES, they find it just as difficult to listen to advice. A particular experience comes to my mind. This entrepreneur told me, "Why should I suddenly start to listen? If I had listened to advice I would not be where I am now and anyway this is only a temporary setback. This is my show and I will see it through till the end."

Type H-ACTIVE entrepreneurs sometimes lead their organizations until they are seriously incapacitated or pass on to that eternal marketplace in the sky. At that stage, a takeover by anyone is very difficult indeed. The heart is cut out of the business and it frequently dies or at best withers for a considerable length of time.

All in all, an H-ACTIVE entrepreneur's commitment is beyond reproach.

ACTIVE

Type ACTIVE entrepreneurs do not have a clear role in their SENIC organization any more. They have handed over to one, two, or even more sons and/or daughters or, less commonly, to the most senior of their trusted managers. They tend to interfere frequently. In the words of one I knew well, "I have to jump in from time to time before things really get out of hand. After all, I know what's right for the business."

Entrepreneurs who have decided to partially withdraw from the business, our ACTIVE type, tend to be torn between being there and not being there. At first it seemed a good idea to hand over the reins, but the chances are that they are not really enjoying their free time. That is not altogether surprising; the business was their life.

ACTIVE entrepreneurs cannot get used to the idea that their informal information circuit does not work as well as it used to because they are no longer involved full time. The most awkward situations do arise when ACTIVEs feel that they need better information. Long live spreadsheets—the ultimate source of data overload! In one case that will always stand out as the ultimate overload, an ACTIVE type entrepreneur received twenty-five glorious pages of spreadsheet data every week. To me he complained bitterly and said, "All these reports don't tell me what's really going on. I'm sure they are hiding stuff from me." When I investigated, I found out from his long-serving and suffering controller that he was never satisfied with what he got but always had more demands for more detailed information. Like a good team player, the controller complied and added another variation on the same theme.

ACTIVE entrepreneurs can suffer badly from the "what will happen when I am not there" syndrome. Unfortunately, this type of on-and-off control is the very reason why the business is "underway but not making way."[4] It sometimes has even started to sink for no clear cut reasons the crew can see. After all, they have not changed anything.

Employees listen to the new family generation or the promoted management, but in the back of their minds they know that at any moment the entrepreneur can step in and reverse a decision. They play it safe by not taking any decisions if they can get away with it. They play what I call the advanced version of the "moi?" game.[5] Sometimes an ACTIVE-type entrepreneur reverts back to type H-ACTIVE. This really does not solve anything, because by picking up the reins full time again he is attempting to turn back the clock. The offspring will have no choice but to accept it, this could be the start of a juicy family crisis, and the newly promoted senior manager effortlessly falls back into his old role. Most of the employees desperately want to think that all will get back to normal and they will live happily ever after again. Nobody really likes change, anyway.

N-ACTIVE

Last but not least, we have Type Not really Active owner-managers. They are the ones that are semi-retired. They drop in when they feel like it, go away on extended holidays, "enjoy" their new-found hobbies, and keep their finger on the pulse by some form of regular (or often irregular) tailor-made management reporting system. Now you, my dear entrepreneur-in-crisis, would no doubt never accept this, but I have seen management reports that were totally devoid of real information and were corrupted expertly by an entrepreneur's closest "yes-men." All they wanted was a quiet life, and some of the tricks to look good and stay out of trouble practiced by these creative but misguided souls would do subsidiary management of a multinational proud. The magnitude is different, but the tricks were the same. (See Time Out 3.3 below.)

It Couldn't Happen to You—or Could It?
TIME OUT 3.3
The Italian Job

This is a story that was related to me by a friend who at that time was an auditor in a team charged by a U.S. parent company to investigate the goings on in their Italian subsidiary. The product was a sticky substance often found on pavements—chewing gum.

A newly appointed managing director (MD) for the Italian subsidiary was soon familiar with the obsession of U.S. companies to grow every quarter by a certain percentage. He also discovered that the financial reporting was somewhat detached from the sales and production reporting, and that the senior VP for finance in the United States would confer only with his Italian controller. He was not involved in those financial discussions at all.

So armed with these facts, the new MD decided to make his subsidiary a shining example to all and make sure that growth in production and sales was guaranteed. He discussed his growth plans with some clients, they hired warehouse space, and whenever he was required to make the numbers look good our MD would ship to these willing clients.

Naturally, accounts receivable got a bit out of hand, but everyone knows that Italians have their own ideas on payment terms. Also, that was a financial problem and nothing to do with sales and production. After his first year in the new job, our Italian MD was duly elected the most successful MD in the Group and was given the medals and the bonuses that we all dream of and aim for.

About six months later, an internal auditor in the United States became suspicious. Growth in Italy never seemed to falter and always came in at about 10 percent each and every month. To make a long story short, the scam was discovered, there was a warehouse full of chewing gum, and our new Italian MD had to look for another job.

More common are simple tricks like invoices printed before the end of the month but shipments made only the next month—arranged with customers so their payment terms are not affected—and an all time favorite: expenses that miraculously become assets.

(For a comprehensive treatment of various accounting tricks, see *Accounting for Growth: Stripping the Camouflage from Company Accounts* by Terry Smith, Random House UK Ltd., 1992.)

So, a real danger for an N-ACTIVE entrepreneur is that the team only tells him what he likes to and wants to hear. That's the downside of an autocratic regime where the autocrat is more absent than present.

The prize for the optimum display of "tell only what the boss wants to hear" was won by an N-ACTIVE entrepreneur from my recent past. He had the annoying habit, though useful for employees, of answering his own questions. He'd say, "We must have lost the account with Mr. X because of the way Sean [the new GM] has dealt with him, don't you think?" Or, "How was your visit to the German plant? Are they still having as much trouble with Product X? Probably still are. These B ... couldn't organize a booze-up in a brewery."

This was pure magic for his long-serving and trusted senior managers. They had developed the agreeable nod and the incoherent mumble to a fine art. If this is not a self-fulfilling prophesy, I don't know what is. Fortunately, this entrepreneur was a rare exception, as you no doubt realize.

Type N-ACTIVE entrepreneur's occasional and ad-hoc interference can be quite dangerous, because they no longer have a good feel for the market, the customers, and even their own organization. Nobody and everybody make so-called decisions. Not surprisingly, employees in these organizations play the ultimate or black belt "moi?" game. When the entrepreneur tries to find out what really went on, a seasoned trial lawyer could learn a thing or two about ducking, diving, slipping, and sliding from these employees!

An example that comes to mind was an N-ACTIVE entrepreneur who after a long period of absence suddenly appeared. He got really upset about a particular decision that was made in his absence. He tried his utmost to find out what had happened but failed, because all he heard was, "It wasn't me that made the decision. Why don't you ask Charlie?" Naturally, Charlie had a similar excuse and referred him to Bob, and so on. His whole management team reacted in this fashion. When he got back to the first "victim" the man said, "I could have sworn Charlie knew." You can't get a better example of the perfectly executed black belt "moi?" game. After a while he gave up in disgust and disappeared for another extended trip. To me he said, "I don't need the money anyway."

After a fleeting visit by type N-ACTIVE entrepreneurs, the organization tends to fall back into blissful slumber until the next time they make an appearance. Organizations led by N-ACTIVE types are without clear guidance, have stagnated, or, worse, are declining. This is particularly dangerous in today's marketplace. SENIC businesses like this are ripe for the takeover, if it is not too late already, or a slow but accelerating demise. A palace revolution would also be an option. But because most of the senior managers have spent a lifetime doing exactly what the entrepreneur wanted, they are not cut out to be rebels. The obedience model inherent in the entrepreneurial organization does not foster a climate of *intrapreneurship*.[6]

In summary, Table 3.1 reflects, perhaps a bit tongue-in-cheek, my three declining phases of entrepreneurs. If you are an entrepreneur, I trust you

Table 3.1
Entrepreneur-in-Crisis Three Phases: Basic Management Behavior

	Leading	Organizing	Delegating	Controlling
Type H-ACTIVE	What a question!	Creative, continually changing, but forthright and spontaneous.	Not really—only the things he doesn't like doing.	And how!!
Type ACTIVE	Yes, but he won't admit it.	No, leaves that to others but reserves the unspoken right to interfere at any time.	Yes to responsibility, no to authority	Yes, but he feels he is losing it.
Type N-ACTIVE	No, but he won't admit it either.	No longer knows what it means.	Nobody knows. Things just seem to happen until his next appearance.	No, but he thinks he has it.

have realized by now that the purpose of this section is to make you understand that you cannot abdicate partly. There are many ways you can be in charge of a business, but you can't run it part-time—and most definitely not during SENIC times. When you really have had enough of it, it's much easier to sell and be done. Plenty of entrepreneurs have opted for selling and sailing in the past. Whether that might be the right solution for you, the current reader entrepreneur, only you can decide.

Correlation between Start-up and Active Types?

It could also be interesting to examine whether the "let go or not let go" elasticity syndrome exhibited by entrepreneurs-in-crisis has a correlation to the very origin of the entrepreneurial phase. How did the company initially succeed?

1. Was it a real vision translated into action?
2. Was it a "good idea" but only a very limited client base agrees?
3. Was it a single-minded effort to get from A to B?
4. Was it an initial attempt from A to B, then a determined, market-inspired change in mid-course to C to find the right niche?
5. Was it just luck and did an entrepreneur stumble onto something in the right place at the right time?
6. Or did a first generation start it? Then perhaps the market the business operated in took off due to an event beyond the players' control during the second or third generation and the business benefited almost automatically. No special effort required initially.[7]
7. Was the first generation relatively happy with a limited scope but then the second generation really wanted to move and shake it?

Now one could also argue that type ACTIVE and N-ACTIVE entrepreneurs are a direct result of reaching the first organizational crisis. If the business is going through a difficult phase, it certainly cannot be much fun for the entrepreneurs. They might react by trying to put distance between themselves and the business. Subconsciously they could be seeking a "sharing of the blame" scenario. After all, failure is a real possibility during SENIC times.

Unfortunately this is a bit out of character for entrepreneurs. I am more inclined to believe that some entrepreneurs have great difficulty in letting go of their overall and totally encompassing leadership role. So they opt for a partial solution in acting as ACTIVE or N-ACTIVE. Particularly during this period of crisis, ACTIVE or N-ACTIVE leads to more confusion than is necessary and certainly overly complicates matters.

The Future Today

Now let me remind you of one of the opening statements of this section: "What can happen if you don't take action." The future for, in particular,

ACTIVE and N-ACTIVE scenarios is not great. The longer you stay in SENIC the more difficult survival becomes. Therefore it is paramount for you to recognize the symptoms and start taking remedial action before it is too late. Whatever you do, plan to get out of the SENIC phase before you become too ACTIVE or fall into N-ACTIVE.

FOULS
- Feeling of losing control.
- Attempting to turn back time.
- Forgetting that ACTIVE and N-ACTIVE probably spell D-A-N-G-E-R.
- Allowing frequent "moi?" games.
- Creating self-fulfilling prophesies.
- Displaying the elasticity syndrome: "To let go or not to let go."

FREE THROWS
- Recognize SENIC for what it is and plan your way out of it.

DON'T LET YOUR MESSAGE GET "LOST IN TRANSLATION"

In the modern world of business, it is useless to be a creative original thinker unless you can also sell what you create. Management cannot be expected to recognize a good idea unless it is presented to them by a good salesperson.

David Ogilvy (1911–1999)

The Importance of Internal Selling

As a business owner, you are quite skilled at selling your ideas to others. During the SENIC onslaught, this skill needs to be used to convince your staff and probably yourself as well into believing that the business can survive. This message needs to be very convincing, but what's more important: it needs to be coupled to tough action as well. That's where the "translation" bit comes in. To believe and act in singular fashion is no longer sufficient. Your business is bigger than you at SENIC and you need to convince your staff, your customers, and other interested parties that in order to progress, "things" have to change. What was in need of change was discussed in Chapter 2, but knowing it, translating it, and doing it are three different things.

Knowing It

To recognize what needs to change is certainly a good start. But do you actually know what needs to change in detail? There are quite a few entrepreneurs in my past who told me that they knew exactly what was needed. When asked to summarize it verbally or put it on paper the answer was often, "it's far too difficult to explain." In my opinion that's not knowing it at all. It's like a student who comes to you and tells you that he has studied a particular text and understands it. When asked a question about the text, his answer is, "I know it but I just can't put it in words!" That's not knowing it at all. Deeper analysis is required to know what has to be done. Thus, thinking you know it and knowing it are two totally different things—in particular because you, the entrepreneur, need to transmit what is required to your whole organization. If you can't define it, you can't transmit it to the very people that need to implement it.

Translating It

Often your message will "get lost in translation" because you have not accepted the fact that you don't know it yourself. Unfortunately, because of the behavioral elements involved, namely your character traits and the "obedience model" that is almost certainly still in operation, there are not many members of staff that will ask for clarification or contradict you. You are always right even if they don't quite understand what you actually want. If you accept this state of affairs you are probably not getting any help from your staff and that's exactly why the many important things that need to change are not changing. The message is left misunderstood or far too ambiguous and hence the required action is not forthcoming.

Doing It

If you think that knowing it and translating it are the difficult parts, think again. Doing it is where the leaders are really separated from the non-leaders. This is the really difficult part because it starts with you, the entrepreneur. There's an awful lot of lip service paid at this stage, in particular when you have tried to change by asking consultants to point you in the right direction. Because never mind how "good and wise" you think the advice is, if you are not capable of implementing it you are on a losing track. Some examples come to mind.

The first one relates to a business that was badly in need of an upgrade in customer perception. The owner was asked to define some principles under which he wanted all his staff to operate, and he came forward with a list of about ten virtues, such as, honesty, integrity, reliability, and so forth. Unfortunately all these virtues were almost exactly the opposite of his daily behavior in his business dealings.

The second example relates to an entrepreneurial business that was advised to get out of the market for widgets. The market was shrinking at an alarming rate. There's nothing as worrisome as getting an increasing share of a shrinking market. Unfortunately the entrepreneur in question decided to persist. He was convinced that the market would pick up again and he would be one of the major players. Unfortunately it never did and his demise was just a matter of time. By the time no one wanted widgets any more, his widgets were probably the best ones on the market!

FOULS

- Not knowing it.
- Not translating it correctly.
- Not doing it at all or doing it half heartedly.

FREE THROWS

- Recognize that knowing it and translating it are difficult, but doing it is the ultimate challenge.

DON'T FORGET THE BIC "C"

Profit in business comes from repeat customers, customers that boast about your project or service, and that bring friends with them.

W. Edwards Deming (1900–1993)

Jack-of-all-trades

In the relentless quest to grow as fast as possible, the original idea is often compromised. Growth at all cost can make sense during the start-up phase, but if definition of purpose and focus are missing, the business will end up as a jack-of-all-trades and master of none. Frequently this phenomenon is demonstrated by many an entrepreneur who has failed to define his customers well or not at all. Often these entrepreneurs think in terms of products, or sometimes even use their facilities as the business criteria. For example, if your basic ingredients are cement, water, sand, and aggregate you can make flower pots, manhole covers, curbstones, concrete steps, and a multitude of other things. That does not mean that all of these activities should be undertaken. Unfortunately it is often during SENIC times that additional activities are tried in order to boost sales and profit. Thus at the very time that focus and customer definition are important, a lot of effort is expended on other activities using the company's facilities. As these activities are often not separated financially, contributions to the bottom line are almost impossible to analyze (see Section "Systems that Dictate Your Business Needs" later in this chapter). Many are the SENIC businesses that make money on some activities and lose it just as fast on some other unrelated ones without knowing it.

Not Listening

The Big C, that is, your customers, are your sole reason for existence. During SENIC times it is too easy to get totally engrossed in staffing problems, policies, procedures, and other internal measures that are required to make your business ready for the next growth phase. But, don't forget to listen and speak to your customers during this period. Naturally, speak to customers about your products or services only. Customers are not really interested in your internal problems—they have their own.

Customers are entitled to receive your full attention, particularly during SENIC. It's not the first time, and won't be the last either, that during SENIC customers are not actively listened to and thus seek alternative suppliers while you are reorganizing and solving those tricky internal problems. When you are done, they might be done with you too!

Lip Service Again and Again

Because of the multitude of large companies that publish and continually advertise their "dedication to customers," it is common for entrepreneurial companies to have similar declarations in their brochures and Web sites. The "mission statement strikes again." Just because it sounds so great doesn't mean that you should immediately rush out and make it your own. There are too many SENIC businesses that proclaim the most wonderful things, but have forgotten that first and foremost, "your existing customers are your mission." If you don't like some of these customers, tough. Find others or define what you consider to be ideal customers and then try and get the latter ones interested in your company. For the time being, your current customers *are your very own customers*,[8] and it's much more powerful to have a few simple statements that you can live up to than "copy" meaningless phrases from industry giants. It's a real waste of time and almost certainly could be used against you if customers would only make the effort to read phrases like that and take them seriously.

Customer Complaints

A last word on customer complaints. What has been said before in Chapter 2, Section "Your Customers Are the Key to Growth," remains as valid as is. Thus take legitimate complaints very seriously indeed. A lot of failures amongst SENIC businesses are recorded because a repeat customer is a novelty. Repeat customers are more than likely happy customers. So if you have very few repeat customers, find out why before it's too late. To lose a customer is easy, to find a new one much more difficult.

Don't think that just because very large organizations often exhibit, in my opinion anyway, a blatant disregard for customers, that you can behave the same. It's a different game for them and the single consumer might not be the "key customer" that she likes to think she is. And just because some of the giants of industry adopt certain practices doesn't mean they are valid for your company and your industry.

As an entrepreneur with a company in SENIC you don't have that sort of luxury. Perhaps some of your customers are trying you because they were fed up with being second-class citizens at a much larger supplier. That's your chance; don't spoil it by not paying attention.

It Couldn't Happen to You—or Could It?
TIME OUT 3.4
Customer Service in Practice

The country is not important, the town is irrelevant, and the name of the bank not significant because I was told that all the banks in that particular country used the same powerful customer service technique. Enter me, a customer. Having received a check for my services the evening before, I decided to drop in at "my bank" the next morning and deposit what was, in my opinion, my well-earned fee. After all we all like to make sure the money is safe in our own account as soon as possible. Banking hours were from 0930 until 1600, to cater for easy access to services for the average working punter no doubt! So there I was, like a good Dutchman, on time at 0928 sharp on a quick deposit mission. It's a curse being Dutch and having this fetish about time, particularly in the country in question. The door of the bank was very much closed, after all I was 2 minutes early, but stuck with a piece of tape on those imposing solid doors was a note. Out of curiosity I decided to look at this note, and to my surprise the hand-written announcement read,

Due to Staff training in progress, this branch will not open until 1030.

When I was joined by another "average" punter, he growled and with a sick sense of humor mumbled, "And I bet you they are talking about customer service too."

FOULS

- Being a jack-of-all-trades.
- Not listening.
- Paying lip service to meaningless principles.
- Having few repeat customers.

FREE THROWS

- Understand that your very own customers are your current mission.
- Use customer complaints as opportunities.

SYSTEMS THAT DICTATE YOUR BUSINESS NEEDS

Not everything that can be counted counts, and not everything that counts can be counted.

Albert Einstein (1879–1955)

Contributions to the Bottom Line

To follow on from the jack-of-all-trades argument in the previous section, it is obviously important to know what contributes to your bottom line. In an ideal world the contribution to the bottom line of various product lines should be computed, but the SENIC entrepreneurial business frequently misses the staff and the skills, for that matter, to carry out this type of exercise. That's quite a dilemma because particularly in difficult times that's exactly what needs to happen. As it is not uncommon in SENIC businesses for various product lines to be shared by common facilities and a flexible workforce, the separation of what makes money and what doesn't is not an easy one for a small organization. Nevertheless, it needs to be extracted because, particularly during SENIC, you need to know. Again, focus and getting better at major activities is probably much better than adding activity after activity. You can't diversify yourself out of trouble and certainly not if you don't even know what contributes and by how much. SENIC requires dedication to the problems at hand, not a "fantastic new" idea that might possibly get you out of trouble.[9]

Overkill

Any number of modern software systems will easily produce the information that we need. But with more sophistication comes more demand on input. Sometimes far too many staff members are employed to process data that is seldom looked at. The 80/20 rule is often flouted here to the detriment of the real purpose of the business.

It might not be the main reason for SENIC failures, but system overkill can contribute significantly to a precarious situation. It's too easy nowadays to get bogged down with all the features of a modern system, thereby forgetting what the purpose of all that data, collected and spit out in a different format, really is.

The Human Factor

Another common mistake made by entrepreneurs is to seek a solution for a system that is not working by throwing a more sophisticated software package at it. Often the problem is not so much the old system that is not working but the discipline to make it perform properly. You can't computerize yourself out of sloppy record-keeping habits. Sloppy will just be multiplied! For example, if your staff fills in their weekly time sheets to allocate costs to various activities as a sort of afterthought at 4 o'clock on a Friday afternoon, your "allocated costs" might not reflect the true picture. Discipline is required, and not a new time-keeping software package. Or, take the junior office person who is told to code the purchase invoices received by maintenance and allocate maintenance hours to jobs, because maintenance has no time and no interest. This junior person cannot really be blamed for the wrong picture that emerges in the detailed "budget against actual" report.

It Couldn't Happen to You—or Could It?
TIME OUT 3.5
Garbage In, Garbage Out

The time is early 1990s and the company is a fast-growing service business using a great number of collection vehicles for servicing a very large customer base. We are talking over 400,000 customers serviced by two hundred employees and fifty vehicles. Challenges in this business included the tasks of designing optimal vehicle routes and keeping track of vehicle costs and customer payments.

About a year before I got involved with the business, the entrepreneur decided to upgrade the existing, fairly basic accounting system into a fully fledged, operations and financial database system. A project team was formed, an IT consultant was hired to advise on the system, and an effort was made to define specifications for the new system based on the owner's demand of wanting to know exactly how much each individual collection would, in his words, "contribute to the bottom line." Moreover, the system "damned well better tell him on a daily basis, otherwise it would be no f ... use to him at all."

The IT in-house consultant, not used to arguing with a forceful entrepreneur, had been on a witch hunt for about six months to find a system that could be amended to incorporate this desire, now referred to as an essential functional specification. In the meantime, as is so often the case, the entrepreneur had lost interest, the new system was taking far too long, and after all life moves on! The software vendor and the in-house consultant were trying to implement the amended system by means of a project team that by now consisted of six outside consultants and the financial controller. The operations manager, marketing manager, and the maintenance manager had long since wriggled their way out of the project team. The poor financial controller was being blamed by the entrepreneur for not having the project cost in hand.

All the controller really wanted was a slightly more modern accounting package. Every payment to the consultants resulted in a major row. The entrepreneur always refused to pay this "ridiculous amount for something he still did not have." The consultants threatened to walk off the job if payment was not made, while the vendor whined in the background that the "stability" of the by-now corrupted package could no longer be guaranteed, and the controller tried desperately to keep the project on track. This was the situation when I arrived.

After having spoken to all the relevant parties, I decided to stop implementation. Now I really made some enemies: the entrepreneur, who told me that he had already spent a fortune and it was better to proceed and finish the job; the consultants, as months of planned lucrative work had been taken away from them; and the vendor, because I refused partial payment for the package.

> It took me some time to explain to the entrepreneur that a system like that would require minute-by-minute input from drivers, mechanics, and even office clerks to convert all the relevant data into meaningful information. What's more, he would need a considerable increase in office staff to process all this data produced by the daily operations or alternatively invest in online portable terminals and training for all his operational staff.

Then there are the countless mistakes that are made because all the data is not captured at source but is transferred via other means like spreadsheets, e-mails, and so forth, because the software routines that would have taken care of automatic transfer were not implemented. False economy!

There are countless examples of software packages in SENIC businesses that are sabotaged without real malice because the data fed into them is not worth the time spent on it. Remember: garbage in, garbage out.

Information that "Goes Up" Only

Data that is supplied by staff and never finds it way back via some sort of useful report is very susceptible to sloppiness. Why would the provider care? He is never held to task and will get more and more careless about providing correct information. If you base some of your decisions on that type of information, you might draw the wrong conclusions. This could be fatal at SENIC.

FOULS
- Letting important activities get all tangled up.
- "Too grand for the job at hand."
- Sloppy procedures.
- Having detail galore, but poor accuracy.
- Allowing no feedback.

YOUR MISSION MUST ALWAYS WALK THE TALK

If I were two-faced, would I be wearing this one?
Abraham Lincoln (1809–1865)

You Have Set the Tone

An important point, which needs to be discussed under the heading of "your mission must always walk the talk," is a must with a capital *M*, whether you like it or not. During the period of your reign you have shaped what can be referred to as the culture of your business. In other words, your behavior has had the biggest impact on the attitudes of your employees and hence the norms and values of your business.

Never mind about mission statements, the vision, written codes of conduct, value statements, and the like. It was and is your behavior, as the business leader, that determines how employees will act and feel about the business, its clients and their own status.

It's Your Actions

Your actual actions will be seen and heard better than any amount of spoken words, like speeches, insincere or even sincerely meant statements, and so forth. This is sometimes referred to as the "lead by example" principle that affects behavior in your organization. Psychologists call this the *social influence theory*.

To quote from an article by Steven Berglas (1977), a consultant psychologist,

> If your employees know you to be corrupt, their attitude towards work will be shaped by what you do, your mission or values statement be damned. When people at the top of an institution behave in a self-centred,

---

It Couldn't Happen to You—or Could It?
TIME OUT 3.6
If These Were the Rules, You Can Guess What the Culture Was!

In the canteen of a medium-sized manufacturing business, about two hundred employees, these *rules* had been on the notice board, obviously for some time. My guess is that the entrepreneur, type N-ACTIVE, had not been in the canteen for a while. Let's call the company EASTLAND.

EASTLAND RULES OF MANAGEMENT

1. Never admit that you are wrong. It's a sign of weakness.
2. When you know that you are wrong, start screaming and performing.
3. Always shout louder than anyone else, threaten a firing, throw a tantrum, and then walk away.
4. If necessary, verbally abuse us. After all, "You must be right."
5. Set targets that are totally unrealistic. Then, when we don't achieve them, remind everyone how "uncommitted" we are.
6. If at all possible, change the production schedule as often as you can at irregular intervals. We do enjoy a challenge!
7. Expect total commitment from all of us for below-average pay.
8. Keep proclaiming that we are screwing you left, right, and center.
9. Still, a lot of good people work here. Makes you wonder, doesn't it?

narcissistic way, their "screw the rules" attitude is likely to be emulated by all they come into contact with.

And further on,

> When you lie and believe there will be no consequences for your leadership status or your bottom line, if your key workers are spineless and mercenary too, then you may be correct. Lawyers will tell you that the courts are so full of pathological prevaricators that judges and arbitrators have come to believe that everyone who stands before them is at least mildly disingenuous. The CEO who lies and cheats, however, should remember this: the liar's punishment is not that he is not believed, but that he can believe no one else. That's the true consequence of amoral leadership.[10]

The culture you set by your actions will last well beyond your own direct personal involvement. It is therefore important to ask yourself, "Is this how I would like to be treated myself?"

It is certainly not too late to influence a culture that is only just emerging in a SENIC business. You, the entrepreneur can help shape it for the future by your actions, not your words.

Be Truthful and Then Persuasive

That's why it is so important as well to live up to your mission statement. Remember the example given in Section "Don't Forget the BIG 'C,'" Lip Service Again and Again. How can your employees live up to something that is just not true? You know it, they know it, the customers would know it if they would have read it, so what's the result? No one but no one, takes it seriously. And if there's one thing that needs to be taken seriously during SENIC, it's your mission, your actions, and your products and services.

FREE THROWS
- Remember: Actions speak louder than words.
- ACTIONS SPEAK LOUDER THAN WORDS.
- Set norms and values realistically, then live by them.

DON'T BE THE CHAMPION RULE BREAKER OR FIRE CHIEF

> Sometimes I lie awake at night and ask, "Where have I gone wrong?" Then a voice says to me, "This is going to take more than one night."
>
> Charles M. Schulz (1922–2000)

It Couldn't Happen to You—or Could It?
TIME OUT 3.7
Lead by Example

It was already dark, six o'clock in the evening. We were all tired and ready to go home. We had been canvassing new clients, door-to-door, for a new recycling service for about a week. If the customer agreed and signed a year's contract we left a brand new container that would be collected at regular intervals. The service was not cheap but we had a fair amount of success that day. One container only was left on the truck. With a team of ten we had been at it for over twelve hours. I said to all of them, "All right, each one of us will have one more go. There's a bottle of whiskey in it for the lucky one who sells the last container today. If not, we'll take it back to the depot. Tomorrow is another day."

So we all tried and we all failed. Just about then, the owner of the company, type ACTIVE, showed up. When he saw the lone bin on the truck and heard the story, he said, "Give it to me. I'll show you how it's done." He went to the next house. It took a while, but he came back minus the container. He said to me, "That's how it's done! You folks couldn't sell beer in a pub. Now let's all go home."

Obviously, we were all suitably impressed. His master's voice had done it again. Where the masses had failed, the master had scored!

A few weeks later, one of the area representatives was busy sorting out some customer issues in that area when a housewife came running up to him. She asked him, "When are you coming to get that container back from me?" When he pleaded ignorance, she explained. Apparently a couple of weeks ago a short, tubby, red-faced gentleman, our very own entrepreneur, had pleaded with her to look after a container for him as he could not take it home. She first refused, but he kept on insisting and gave her £10 for her trouble. He told her he would be back in the morning to collect it but never came!

A Simple Example

As you, the entrepreneur reader, might have gathered by now, I have spent a lot of my time in construction, manufacturing, and engineering type companies. Most of these organizations require their employees to wear, amongst other protective items, hard hats. Nowadays you can't enter a building site, factory, or engineering works or you are greeted by these imposing signs that proclaim in no uncertain terms that: This is a Hard Hat Area, High Visibility Jackets Must Be Worn, Protective Footwear Must Be Worn, and so forth. You can guess what I am aiming at; obviously the small print on these signs should have stated, "This does *not*, repeat *not*, apply to the entrepreneur/owner." Presumably the right to decide what to do on your own premises is deeply ingrained in the entrepreneurial culture.

I can also quote you many similar examples in office environments, such as giving credit to a customer while the rule for the organization is no credit is given at any time, giving price reductions while the "death penalty" is threatened to any salesperson who even thinks about this concept, or no personal withdrawals from inventory while taking any amount of goodies yourself. Such behavior is incredibly demotivating for the staff.

Instant Procedures

In the same category fall the "procedures" that are made, forgotten, made again but different, forgotten again, reintroduced, and so on. Thus you get this type of conversation: "I thought the procedure was to always fit lifting hooks," "No, that was the procedure but now we want clients to specify it." Thus the poor client is confronted with a new procedure and wasn't even aware there was a procedure for "to fit or not to fit a lifting hook" because it was another client who complained that she didn't want lifting hooks in the first place!

Rule Breaking

All these instances refer to the very satisfying habit, for you the entrepreneur at least, of rule breaking. Now some of you might say, rules are there to be broken, so what's the problem? The problem is that that type of expression refers to the much larger organizations where the rules often stifle initiative and employees hide behind them. You don't quite fall into this category as yet, so give the rules—that you probably made yourself—a chance. Regrettably if you, the entrepreneur, are the champion rule breaker, the rest of the organization thinks that these rules are not really "those sort of rules" anyway. Or as one employee once said to me, "I didn't think Norman [the entrepreneur] actually meant it!" So before you know it you have a whole lot of little entrepreneurs being inventive and bending rules to the breaking point, probably at your expense. If you then suddenly decide to come down hard and read everyone the riot act, the behavior of all your employees will change again. Now even the most trivial of decisions lands on your desk. No one makes any decisions at all until you tell them in no uncertain terms, "to stop acting the fools and get on with it," and that'll be the end of round one. Then you, the champion rule breaker, is observed breaking another one of your own rules and round two is ready to start— not very conducive to day-to-day operations at all and even less productive during SENIC times!

Fire Fighting

In terms of level of contentment, fire fighting must rate as one of the most agreeable activities in post-entrepreneurial companies. I'm convinced that the cell phone has made fire fighting in organizations an even more intense and satisfying experience. What do I actually mean by this? Fire fighting is the habit of trying to do a great number of things simultaneously, but in reality doing very little and certainly not completing any of the tasks at hand. Those most intrusive of modern gadgets, the cell phone and the incoming e-mail alert, must rate as excellent contributors to modern fire-fighting tactics. Nothing seems to be more important, even during the most intense conversations, than the call of the cell phone. Before you know it, you, the participant in a face-to-face, real-life conversation, must take second place to the caller.

But fire fighting was around well before the cell phone or e-mails became commonplace. No doubt, these gadgets have added to the intensity of the experience, but unplanned activities, customer complaints, faulty products, unscheduled deliveries, rush jobs, frequent tool changes, interrupted production runs to cater for whatever, and so forth have always managed to disturb what probably never was a solid routine but has now become so disruptive that almost anything requires the "fire brigade."

Fire-Fighting Origins

The reason for fire fighting is often found in the very essence of the entrepreneurial start-up phase where "everything was possible," and the "can do" attitude prevailed. You didn't have that many clients and by working yourself and your team very hard, you could satisfy them all. Unfortunately when the business is successful and gets larger and SENIC is reached, lack of planning, mistakes, special customer requests, and lack of routine and procedures can no longer be tolerated without consequence. That's when the fun starts—Superman to the rescue or firefighting in "real time." Unfortunately it's very addictive but oh so satisfying, the rushing about, the waving of arms, the flashing lights, the urgent e-mails, the constant phone calls, the last minute changes, or the urgent deliveries. "Get it sorted out" is the slogan and boy do your staff take that message to heart!

It's very difficult to get out of fire-fighting routines, and not because they appear to be very rewarding, but because they are ingrained in your SENIC organization from the recent past. At SENIC stage, your busy and dynamic entrepreneurial environment has turned into disorganized chaos and you, the entrepreneur, are in charge of it all!

FOULS
- Having rules for everyone but yourself.
- Having too many procedures. ("These are the procedures. If you don't like them we've got others.")
- Believing that fire fighting is productive.
- Creating "dynamic" environments.

YOUR KEY STAFF MIGHT NOT BE UP TO THE TASK

The man who goes alone can start today; but he who travels with another must wait till that other is ready.

Henry David Thoreau (1817–1862)

Three Types

We will now return to your most valuable asset that can turn into your SENIC nightmare, namely, your staff. Recall: Every business is as good as the people it employs. Unfortunately, the people that were eminently suitable to be part of your embryonic venture are not often suitable to lead departments in a larger organization. The Peter Principle is very much a major impediment to growth and, less often recognized, is also the reason why new employees don't stay too long. Remember the three types—inner and outer circle and expand-contract—discussed in Chapter 2, Section "Your Staff Is a Close Second." The first two categories, inner and outer circle, are particularly in evidence at the supervisory level of the SENIC business.

Rank and File

During the SENIC phase, the rank and file of the company appear not to care and adopt an attitude of, "I am just doing my job; nobody tells us anything anymore and nothing will change for us anyway." Lately, their requests for sometimes minor changes in working conditions or equipment upgrades have fallen on deaf ears, and they feel totally disassociated from you and your circle of supervisors. Salespeople avoid the office and you won't be able to catch customer-service personnel, the ones with the pickups or the vans, for love nor money. These are the employees who have freedom of movement and their defense to all this SENIC nonsense is "to go it alone" as much as possible. The common feeling amongst them is: As long as we do our job, no one will bother us.

It's almost as if a mentality of "us and them" has developed. The entrepreneur has lost contact and control, is never available for a problem, changes priorities almost daily, and disregards the concept of efficiency. Inner- and outer-circle managers appear to have developed short fuses, and whatever camaraderie was there in the past has long since been lost. So the rank and file who can't flee the office put their noses to the grindstone, execute orders in almost parrot-like fashion, and do what is asked of them. Fortunately there is plenty of overtime available—there always is in a dynamic environment—and with a bit of luck their jobs will be safe. These employees have been on the receiving end of the inner- and outer-circle management for some time and know that arguing or reasoning with the supervision is a waste of time. Blind obedience is much easier!

Even in these difficult SENIC circumstances, the rank and file know damned well who is a real manager and who is a make-believe one. It's a pity that these employees don't often share their stories and experiences with you, the entrepreneur. It would certainly be an eye-opener to listen to their revelations. What's more, it would save a lot of time. But unfortunately, management at SENIC by unsuitable inner- and outer-circle employees is seen as being executed with your full approval, and who are they to complain? They only want to do the job and are perhaps even a bit bitter that they have not been selected for "higher" things. After all, they wonder what it actually is the "supervision" does. One thing is almost for certain, they don't really supervise because they probably don't know how!

Peter Principle in Action

Thus promotion of unsuitable inner- and outer-circle employees often leads to undesirable situations like the ones described next.

In one of my assignments, many years back, the technical services staff of a SENIC engineering company always used to joke with each other when confronted with a tricky problem and trying to decide who should solve it. One would ask, "If the answer is Larry?" And the other would answer, "The question is wrong!" Then they would burst out laughing. Larry was their inner-circle supervisor of many years standing who, I found out some time later, had not lifted nor seen a screwdriver since he was promoted to a supervisory position quite a while ago by his friend, the entrepreneur in question.

In another case, in a twenty-four-hour production environment, I noted that the night and weekend shifts were particularly popular. It took a while for me to find out why, but one of the weekend supervisors told me in a weak moment: "That's when Sherlock and Holmes are not around, so we can get on with our work." Sherlock was the nickname for the production manager and Holmes was his administrative assistant. Apparently they were real nitpickers. A classic example of an inner and an outer circle, they were pals of this particular entrepreneur, never ready to compliment, but ever so fast to pick up on minor mishaps.

Then there's the case of the "promoted" accountant who became the financial controller. His staff used to start at nine and leave at four each and every day. They always had time for coffee and a chat while he, their boss, worked all hours of the day and went home every night with a bunch of documents under his arm. When asked why he did not delegate some of his work, he looked almost surprised and said, "I am the only one who can do this properly"—another case of a good accountant turned into a lousy manager; the Peter Principle strikes again. His staff knew all right what he was like and used it to their own advantage to lead the easy life. They had almost made it a sport to see how much work they could give their boss before he would break.

And then there was the sales manager who had a sales meeting only once a quarter. When it was suggested to him that more frequently would more than likely be required from now on, he said to me, "But it's so difficult to get them together because they all have their own schedules. I don't really want to interfere." Lovely, isn't it? The salespeople had been running rings around him since his appointment some years back. Still desperate to be accepted as one of them, he was totally incapable of holding them to task.

Yes, bad management affects all employees and the SENIC business will have more than its fair share of it. At this stage of the game it's not easy for you, the entrepreneur, to overcome the cynicism and apathy of the rank and file. After all it's your inner- and outer-circle supervisors that are most likely at fault. But remember the rank and file are the actual people that make the product, provide the service, and give the support. This is where the work is done or, undone if one is not careful. Surely they do deserve to be led properly?

The Company's DNA

The very DNA that you, the entrepreneur, liked so much in your own "merry band," the inner- and outer-circle employees, the dedication, long hours, flexibility, and commitment has now reached its limit and is starting to work against you, and all because these very loyal and dedicated employees are probably totally unsuitable to lead others. Instead of helping you to run the business "on the foot plate" they are effectively operating the brakes from the "guard van" and slowing you down without you knowing it. Your best salesperson is not necessarily an effective sales manager, your trusted and hard-working team leader probably makes a lousy production manager, and your star-performing warehouse clerk doesn't know how to supervise four aspiring "stars." The predominant entrepreneurial management style, what I refer to as the benevolent dictatorship, hasn't helped to hone their management skills either! So your greatest asset, your people, has turned into a significant liability, your ineffective management team.

Structure

Although an attempt has been made to appoint inner- and outer-circle employees to positions of responsibility, their unsuitability and your management style has only added to the level of confusion so typical at SENIC times. The old systems of doing things and involving people at random are much more powerful than any system suggested by a consultant or superimposed by you. By promoting some people to positions that sound important but have not really been properly defined you are adding to the confusion and, let me add, your overhead without getting the real benefit of management that is so urgently required. The structure of your company needs to be changed to cater to a higher level of business activity. Sound, dependable performance is required in order to achieve continued customer satisfaction. With growth the realization must come that you can no longer travel alone, but have to travel in company—that is, teamwork is required.

FOULS
- Fostering the Peter Principle.
- The rank and file adopting an "us and them" mentality.
- Letting supervision be just overhead than real value-adding activity.
- Allowing "freedom of movement" employees to come and go at will.
- Letting the workforce become passive.
- Letting the company's structure survive well past its "sell by" date.

FULL ORDER BOOKS, BUT ...

I'm living so far beyond my income that we may almost be said to be living apart.

e.e. cummings (1894–1962)

Believe It or Not, Cash Flow Once Again

It's so eminently logical, but in the age of seemingly endless credit, where even individual consumers[11] are encouraged to spend beyond their means, it is not surprising that many a business is "floored" by overextending their credit limit with no obvious way out. Cash flow might be the cause of the demise; the symptoms must be recognized in order to tackle the illness. The cause of a prolonged, sometimes fast but often deadly, cash-flow crisis can be found in what one could consider positive and negative SENIC symptoms—positive in the sense that you have most elements of your business under control but your success is totally unchecked as yet, and negative because you have no real control because you are falling down on one of the basics.

Positive SENIC Symptoms

Under the positive symptoms, the most common one is without a doubt the success of the initial product offering. Demand is so great and the desire of the entrepreneur to grow so strong that the business starts living beyond its means. Ever greater production runs demand more supplies, more overtime, and so forth, but cash is not as fast incoming as supplies and wages are outgoing. Some stop measures, such as invoice discounting, can be used, but they further dilute actual earnings. If working capital finance is already up to your nostrils, a hiccup in production, or an unexpected, albeit temporary, drop in sales will lead to drowning. Then you will discover that banks are not the real friends of small but growing SENIC companies.

Another common positive SENIC symptom is fast growth of an easily copied product that is difficult to protect by means of a patent.[12] As soon as the much bigger competition finds out that you are making a dent in their market share, the full might of the bigger players is brought to bear, resulting in some sort of price war. But you can't afford a price war; you don't have the diversity of products or the financial muscle that the larger players possess. Lower prices will destroy your cash flow as you are not yet geared up for larger production runs or serious marketing expenditures. What's more, you don't have a reputation. All you have done is started a new race, but you are being overtaken once you are beyond the starting line and trying to gather pace. Of course, there have been and will be entrepreneurs who will beat those terrible odds. Those are the ones who write the entrepreneurial books that we all rush out to buy to "discover the secret of success," thus making the rich even richer. Success is not that easily copied in your own world, and for most of you the cash-flow squeeze will do just that and make your promising start run into great difficulty, unless you *passionately manage your rate of growth and so your cash flow.*

Negative SENIC Symptoms

You might well ask that if the positive symptoms lead to great difficulty, what do the negative ones do? The negative ones lead to the same difficulty. After all, "lack of money" has no color, creed, or other features. But as far as symptoms go, the negative SENIC symptoms relate to something that is inherently flawed in your business. Let me give you some examples.

The most common of the negative ones is not chasing your payments due persistently and actively. I have come across businesses whose credit terms were 30 days but the actual position was more like 160 days. There's always a "good" reason. Some customers just don't pay if you don't pursue them continually. Or, remember the excuses of the salespeople who don't want to spoil their cherished customer relations by getting involved in that lowest of all activities, chasing the money? Other common negative symptoms are often related to not reacting quickly to what are often minor difficulties with your product. Particularly in manufacturing, engineering, and construction environments, this is a common reason for customers to delay large payments. Put it right and demand your payment. Remember my definition of a customer: "Someone who buys your product and pays for it."

Negative SENIC symptoms also occur when more than one product line is part of the customer offering. The sales for each product line are recognized most of the time but costs are not really allocated correctly. The entrepreneur has made some initial pre-calculations to show that good margins can be made on each new line, but actual costs are not allocated properly and post-calculations are seldom carried out. After all, facilities, equipment and human resources are shared, purchases are not differentiated, and everyone helps themselves from stock, and so forth. All is well until the cash flow spins out of control. Now where do you start looking? Is it the initial product offering, the second line, or the brand new line that takes everyone's time and has a disproportioned level of rejects? Every one involved has a theory but where are the facts?

Another common negative SENIC symptom is not unlike the previous one but with a juicier and potentially even more spectacular consequence, namely, early diversification without interrelation. The entrepreneur that appears to be doing well in the one business gets involved in another dissimilar one, then another one, and perhaps even another one. These businesses although totally unrelated are often interrelated in terms of cash flow, because they share resources, purchases, and a lot of other things, not to mention the time and scattered attention of the entrepreneur. The excuse for this loose control is often that newly acquired activities cannot yet stand alone. This is an accepted principle in the corporate world but not really applicable to three or four entirely unrelated businesses that are trying to get off the ground. So the net result is a mixed cash flow that gets out of control but no one knows why anymore. Was it the original manufacturing business or the second one acquired in a different location, or the hotel or the real estate portfolio, or perhaps the book store? If these businesses are eventually separated financially, what often shows up is that the original business had not yet reached sufficient maturity to generate good steady profits to finance other activities. Also, purchase controls were not in place to allocate costs where they were really incurred—so busy, busy, busy, running from the one to the other, spending hours with account clerks to try and separate some of the costs, querying invoices, refusing to sign supplier payment checks. In other words, real fire-fighting activities but very difficult to regain control.

Then there's the reverse case. All the various activities are very well monitored, but the number of clerks that keep it all nice and tidy is way over the top for the small business. Everyone is very busy again, this time correctly allocating all costs but the profit margin on the various activities is not enough to sustain that particular level of overhead. Get overhead back to what you can afford, limit your reporting requirements to essentials by practicing the 80/20 rule, or perish as an exceptionally well-documented and organized business that will soon be laid to rest.

In all of the previous examples the order books are full, the business appears to be thriving, everyone is terribly busy, but control over your own destiny has been lost. Regain it as soon as possible or suffer the inevitable consequences. You won't be the first business that goes down with a full order portfolio. Whether the revenue commissioners, your suppliers, or your banks close you down is just semantics.

FOULS
- Permitting uncontrolled growth.
- Developing products too easy to copy.
- Having too many product lines.
- Diversifying early without strict control.

FREE THROWS
- Manage your rate of growth.
- Differentiate your products.
- Control and allocate your costs properly.
- Know your overhead and control it.

YOUR VENTURE IS NOT "THE FAMILY BENEVOLENT SOCIETY"

Where there's a will there's a relative.

> Old Irish Proverb

Early Family Interest

During the early entrepreneurial years, your family tends to play a minor role in the affairs of the new venture. Most members of your extended family adopt a wait-and-see approach. Once the business reaches the SENIC stage, the chances are that the precariously thought of endeavor could transform itself also into an embryonic family business. Family members are starting to show, and what's more, express an interest, because it really looks like your business is going somewhere and continuity is proving to be a real option. The first signs of the family's attention are more than likely focused on securing employment for some of its members. So an important, perhaps even the most important, ingredient, the family, is added to your SENIC business at a time when turmoil and change are the order of the day and even survival might be at stake.

From now on, the greatest influencing factor on your behavior will probably be your family. The achievement of getting a venture off the ground has been noticed by all your relatives, close and distant ones alike. They have changed their tune from ignoring it, to being mildly interested, to making statements like, "I thought some time ago that he was onto something." Family functions, particularly those organized by you, are well attended, and the jockeying for position, or favors, is well under way.

At this stage you are adored by most members of your family, ignored by some, but envied by all. Some entrepreneurs have even started to behave like the head of the family and virtually seem to fulfill the role of the Don or Patriarch. They appear willing to do just about anything to keep the family together, even to the detriment of their business.

Perhaps this is a subconscious desire by entrepreneurs to re-acquire what was lost through what Collins and Moore (1970) described as "role deterioration." What transpired from their study of 150 entrepreneurs was an image of tough and hard-nosed individuals that were almost obsessed from an early age by a powerful need for achievement and independence. At some point in their lives, they all faced disruption that appeared to trigger the start of setting out on their own: "They interwove their dilemmas into the projections of a business. In moments of crises they did not seek a situation of security. They went on into deeper insecurity."[13]

This is interesting and might explain why you, an entrepreneur of a SENIC business, behave as you do towards your family even at the chance of endangering your own mission and the business. So, perhaps this all-powerful motive to never again be confronted by your own experiences of disruption, coupled with your newfound importance within the family, enables all other members to get a slice of the action without unduly having to prove themselves.

Business vs. Family

If family norms and aspirations would be the same as the norms and vision for the business, all would be well. Unfortunately, family and business norms are almost without fail at odds because they tend to be direct opposites. Whereas a family can be considered to be a closed system and almost certainly emotionally based, the SENIC business, like any business, operates in an open system, focusing on markets, customers, and effective operations. Membership in an organization is voluntary and can be terminated at will, but family membership is not a choice or an option and it's for life, whether one likes it or not.

Family members and sometimes close friends in need of a job are put in positions irrespective of their ability to fulfill the role in question, never mind that this, almost inevitably, has a detrimental effect on business efficiency. The worst scenario is one in which a family member is introduced to a specially created position that totally baffles the existing organization. If an entrepreneur feels that there might be resistance from his management, the family member placement just happens. No introduction, no explanation, and no justification—James the brother or Bob the cousin just arrives! Suddenly, all other employees are totally ignored in order to accommodate a new family member. As most entrepreneurs do not write memos, it is left up to a trusted sidekick to create the new position with its appropriate title and some vague responsibilities.[14] Welcome to the world of family socialism!

These family appointees get paid, most of the time, according to their private needs and fall totally outside the existing remuneration structure. Naturally, everyone knows this but no one dares to argue. It's not very motivational for non-family employees.

And so it is almost predictable that when family values and business values are mixed by an entrepreneur, conflict is the result. Family socialism and business capitalism will clash time and time again unless specific action is taken. These initial family employment issues are only the first skirmishes.

Particularly during the first revolutionary crisis, this type of conflict between the family and the business can do untold damage. Attention is diverted, business problems take second place, and the organization suffers a considerable setback. The issues around the family are more than likely some of the critical ones that determine whether the business conquers the

It Couldn't Happen to You—or Could It?
TIME OUT 3.8
Of Eyes and Ears and Spies to Match

This type N-ACTIVE entrepreneur, let's call him Mac, had manufacturing plants in a number of countries. One of the plants employed about 150 people and had been doing badly for some time. Mac had spent some time at this plant himself, "to sort things out," with a twenty-five-year-old niece, Emily, who had recently completed a business course.

After a few weeks in the saddle, our type N-ACTIVE got bored and left again to pursue his leisure activities. Emily was left behind to do whatever it was that Emily did. Some of the inner-circle managers in the plant realized that Emily was a direct line to Mac and latched onto her in shameless fashion to seek political and sometimes other favors.

Emily, not yet streetwise, did not recognize this behavior and actually enjoyed the attention that was lavishly showered upon her. In a sense, the whole plant had adopted a culture of deception and gossip—particularly with head office personnel—and of course the blame game. After all it beats working and is much more intriguing and entertaining. Needless to say, the sitting Managing Director had been reduced to a spectator's role with signing authority. This scenario had been in operation for about six months when I was asked to take charge.

In my initial round of interviews with the managers and the staff, I naturally came across Emily. When I asked her what she did for a living, she answered coyly, "I am the eyes and ears of Mac." On my best behavior I tried to explain to her that I did not think that being "the eyes and ears of Mac" was a job as such and I would gladly fit her in as a management trainee to start her career in the business. She refused and told me that only Mac could change her "assignment." Being far too busy to let such a minor incident cramp my style, I forgot about it and ignored Emily. Pretty soon though, I caught on to the prevailing plant culture of gossip and the endless "moi?" games. I discussed this with the sitting management team and told them in no uncertain terms that we were all here to work, responsibility was to be taken and authority given, gossip was not part of the brief, and we, as the management, would deal with facts only. A couple of days later, now having been in the job for all of fourteen days, I got a phone call from Mac, who summoned me to his house for an urgent meeting.

During the ensuing meeting Mac told me that Emily was very unhappy. When I told him that that did not surprise me because she did not have a job, he retorted "but she is my eyes and ears." What followed was a heated and lengthy discussion on my comparing "his eyes and ears" with spying, my instructions to the management team about communicating with head office, gossip in particular, and the reintegration of Emily into the senior management team.

As all these were not negotiable in my book, we reached stalemate quite quickly, but the meeting lasted for well over six hours.

first revolutionary crisis and can achieve longer-term success or, alternatively, keeps on lingering until some of the family issues are settled. In one of my jobs, the entrepreneur, type ACTIVE, took three months to listen and realize that his nephew, son of his favorite sister, was downright lazy and totally unsuited for the position he was appointed to. I think he rather put up with my incessant requests to remove him than face his sister!

Now for most of us, family ties are very important, but to mix family wants with business requirements might jeopardize non-family staff relations as well. A culture of family patronage and blind obedience does not tend to attract and, what is even more crucial, retain the required "bold and bright" non-family employees.

Rules for Business and Family

It is really essential that some rules and regulations are developed for the interface between the business and the family. And if you think you don't need those and you and your family are "not like that," here's a quote from the special report on Family Business in *The Economist* that should help you make up your mind:

> It should be no surprise then, that some 70% of those attending the annual meeting of the Family Firm Institute in Boston in early October (2004) were family therapists. The army of consultants that has sprung up to help family firms resolve differences has its roots deeply sunk in psychoanalysis.[15]

At the moment, the business is still a relatively small unit. The sooner you, the entrepreneur, decide on the structure of the involvement of the family in the business, the earlier a lot of problems and heartaches can be avoided, not to speak of the likely and substantial future psychoanalysts' fees.

FOULS
- Forgetting that where there's a will there's a relative.
- Allowing no-questions-asked job placements for family members and for friends.
- Letting family socialism take precedence over business capitalism.

FREE THROWS
- Put family members through the same hiring process that you would non-family members.
- Never forget you are running a business—not a job service for family members who can't find a place elsewhere.
- Recognize your own desire to assume head-of-family status and beware the pitfalls involved.

NOTES

1. Failure is not necessarily bankruptcy but could also be a significant downsizing of the whole business, or what's perhaps even worse, a continued and prolonged battle to hang on to what is a slow and painful demise until the owner eventually decides to close down.

2. Why in a weak moment? Because in almost all the entrepreneurial businesses I have been associated with, if there was a small employee stake, the entrepreneurs were invariably trying to buy it back.

3. Attribution bias: The tendency of people to credit themselves unduly for successes that are heavily influenced by external factors, such as a boom market or a technology revolution, while disproportionately blaming their failures on external factors.

4. A very apt description "borrowed" from the Regulations for Preventing Collisions at Sea. Making way is moving forward, under way is that as well, plus stopped in the water or even moving astern.

5. *Moi* is the French word meaning "me." It needs to be said with conviction and with a surprised, almost ignorant and hurt look. It is particularly effective if at the same time you cross one or both of your arms in front of your upper body and point to the people standing next to you—also known as the "everybody and nobody are responsible" principle adapted from the civil service or the "now you see them now you don't" theorem from babes in the wood.

6. *Intrapreneurship* is a term used to describe entrepreneurial thinking by employees within organizations.

7. To my mind a classical example of this was the condom industry. Almost dead due to the invention of the birth control pill, the industry was resurrected by the onslaught of AIDS. Even governments are advertising for the product group, with no cost to the industry!

8. Do remember the golden rule: payment for products or services is part of the customer profile.

9. Read Chapter 5, "When a Nightmare Turns into Real Life Madness," for a real-life example of taking one's eye off the ball.

10. By Steven Berglas, "Liar, Liar, Pants on Fire," *Inc. Magazine* (August 1, 1997): 1, www.inc.com/magazine/19970801/1295.html.

11. According to the latest economic indicators (2006) the level of average individual debt in countries like the United States, the United Kingdom, Ireland and many others, runs well above average individual income levels at about 115 to 150 percent.

12. And even if you have a patent, can you afford to defend it?

13. Collins, J. C. and Moore, D. G., *The Organization Makers* (New York: Appleton-Century Crofts, 1970), 134.

14. This must sound familiar to staff in large corporations. In these outfits, it is unofficially called "a political appointment" and the Vice President of Human Resources can justify this appointment in the most eloquent of prose. That's where the education and years of complying with the system pays off!

15. Special Report, "Family Businesses; Passing on the Crown," *The Economist* (November 4, 2004): 2.

4

Creating Order from Chaos

Se vogliamo che tutto rimanga com'e bisogna che tutto cambi.
Freely translated this means, "Everything must change, so that every-
thing stays the same."
In *Il Gattopardo* by Giuseppe Tomasi di Lampedusa (1896–1957)

INTRODUCTION

If you are going through hell, keep going.
Sir Winston Churchill (1874–1965)

If after reading the previous chapters you are still determined to beat the
odds and move your business through SENIC and beyond, let's discuss
what business steps need to be taken to "follow on" from your successful
term as an entrepreneur. The previous discussions on symptoms and causes
have been crucial to recognize and acknowledge SENIC (Still Evolving, Now
in Crisis). It's also beneficial to consider common failures with care to avoid
some of the more serious pitfalls, but now it's time to move on and accept
that, as a matter of fact, the crisis was unavoidable and start taking action.

Get beyond SENIC

Yes, it's true there have been and will be very successful entrepreneurs
that keep on being entrepreneurs. They often leave a flourishing business
behind; appoint a general manager and move on to another venture.
There's nothing stopping you from doing that as well, but first your current
venture needs to be put on a firm footing. It must make steady progress
and provide acceptable returns, that is, you must make it flourish! If you
need permanent help at this SENIC stage and your business can support it,
read Appendix E about recruiting a general manager. But even that won't
let you off the hook. It's your business and you need to attend to it. A good
general manager can certainly help you get the business beyond SENIC to
the next level of activity, but don't make the mistake of abandoning or even
abdicating. Abdication was discussed in some detail in Chapter 3, Section

"Know Your Own Strength (and Weaknesses), as being the main character-istic of entrepreneurs of type N-ACTIVE. Businesses led by N-ACTIVE type entre-preneurs don't go anywhere in a hurry so abdication is a firm no-no, in my book anyway. If you want to abandon, get the business sorted first and then sell, because a business in SENIC ain't worth much, believe me.

No Pain No Gain

Although it's never nice to hear during the crisis, the first organizational crisis is a real-life business test. The test is whether you are actually capable of running a bigger business, adjust your behavior accordingly, and move the business and yourself from strength to strength. Don't stop being an entre-preneur altogether—just add a certain amount of management skills to your repertoire. There are quite a few entrepreneurs who made it beyond SENIC times that will admit to having really learned how to run a business during this challenging period. In the process they learned something as well about their own strengths and weaknesses. If your own weaknesses preclude you from being an effective manager, then at least you know where you must strengthen your organization. Your entrepreneurship combined with an effective general manager is a powerful combination that is very hard to beat.

Now some of you who are part of an industry that has seen tremendous growth might even start thinking that all that talk about SENIC is some-what exaggerated. You probably recall some minor difficulties that were quickly sorted by your own superior talents, a walk in the park—a blip on your company's otherwise unblemished record. You might even have grown your business way beyond what you would consider the entrepre-neurial years. Have I got news for you! Real boom times often hide short-comings, disorganization, and your own entrepreneurial management style until the market turns, and turn it will. Then the odds are that SENIC will clobber you effectively in all its conventional predictability. It might really hurt you, too, if you are not prepared, because you thought you had "made it." The old adage "no pain no gain" must unfortunately be fulfilled in organizational terms as well.

Overreaction

Another important point to remember is not to overreact. Don't throw the baby out with the bathwater, so to speak. If you need to make adjust-ments to your cost pattern, consider them carefully. It's the easiest thing in the world to cut costs, but more difficult to determine what needs to be cut and where. Similarly it sounds easy enough to start saying "no" to custom-ers in order to pick and choose what you want to do, particularly in boom times. But again, are you telling the right customers? It's easy to lose a customer, and more difficult to get him back! Lay off staff—sure, it sounds simple, not so simple in practice because last in first out might not be the best policy to keep your best employees to overcome SENIC conditions. It all revolves around the where, what, and above all HOW questions that

It Couldn't Happen to You—or Could It?
TIME OUT 4.1
Oh, for Those Good Old Days

There were quite a few instances where an entrepreneur, this one with a general manager, showed that for them the transition was very difficult as well.

This "owner with a manager," named Pete, type H-ACTIVE, was in construction. He had been trying to get used to his new role, executive chairman, for a few months. His main role was to network, get agreement on development projects with all the relevant parties, and seek or bid on suitable sites for development work. He always was a networker par excellence. Things were going quite well actually, in my opinion.

One morning I arrived very early at one of the building sites and who was there, helmet, boots, yellow jacket, and all, yelling at one of the foremen? My executive chairman.

From a distance, I bellowed, "Good morning, Pete. What are you doing here?" He turned his head, noticed me, looked somewhat taken aback, then recovered and roared back, "Just wanted to remind myself what it was like."

were discussed in Chapter 2, Section "Decide on What You Want." This very topic will be further discussed in this chapter's Section "Where, What, and Above All HOW."

Good Old Times

Some entrepreneurs will express a great desire to return to the business they had a few years back when it all appeared so easy. The human brain has tremendous capacity to block out past hardships and recall the good times only. First of all, times were probably not as good as you think you remembered them. And secondly, you can never turn back the clock. A business cannot be "tuned down" to what you thought it was some years back. In terms of sales or profits, perhaps, but not with all the ingredients that made the business what it was then. So forget it! This is *now* and you need to face *now* in order to have a business tomorrow.

Reduce If You Like

If you feel that you had enough, "You don't want to play anymore and you want your ball back," and the larger business scene is nothing for you, the best you can do is decide on the bits of the business you want to keep, why and how you want to keep them, and then go for it. Again the same questions, that is, where, what, and how need to be answered. There is never an easy way out, but a well-planned reduction in size might be your answer. You can also beat SENIC by stopping to evolve and reduce instead. Consider it seriously. Probably for most of you this opting out scenario is not really an option, thus on to … *action*. Action—so now it's time to discuss how to arrive at "life after chaos." It's not as complex as it sounds, and not as easy as you think. It's not instantaneous and might take quite some time. Priority, dosage, and timing of change are very important in combination with keeping one's eye firmly on the ball. And don't forget the SENIC slogan, "The Best Is Yet to Come."

FREE THROWS
- Commit yourself. No abdication.
- Plan changes carefully.
- Don't throw the baby out with the bathwater.
- Remember: Good old times are just that.
- Create well-thought-out action plans with action.

COPING WITH CHANGE

Tough times never last. Tough people do.

Robert H. Schuller (1926–)

Prioritize

Possibly the most important principle associated with getting beyond SENIC is to get the short-term goals right before you look beyond. That's perhaps the single most important thing to remember. SENIC can be beaten by getting the short-term goals right and prioritizing what short-term goals are critical. No doubt these goals are also associated with your business's Critical Success Factors (CSFs). There's little point in having a fantastic vision and a well-thought-out and documented five-year plan when your cash flow is telling you that you can't afford to pay next month's wages. To cope with change you really have to set some short-term goals and prioritize. So never mind lamenting about the good old days, talking about what would have happened if …, feeling sorry for yourself, and a host of other "soft" issues. Instead, determine the short-term goals and take the appropriate *action*. No doubt you will agree that the most critical action to be taken is, wait for it, talk to your customers, the Big C.

The Big C

The search for life beyond SENIC must always start with your customers. Peter Drucker (1985) expressed the functions of the firm as follows: "Because its purpose is to create a customer, the business has two—and only—two functions, marketing and innovation. Marketing and innovation produce results; the rest are costs."[1]

Although this sounds patently obvious, it is just as well to remind yourself of this purpose before you start tinkering with your organization in earnest. Customers will tell you soon enough whether your product offering is still desirable, well made and competitive, and whether the service is acceptable. Visits to key customers often point also to the major weakness in your organization. Is it quality, production itself, logistics, or sales office response times? Impress on everyone in the business from yourself to the cleaners that "Customers pay our wages, so let's treat our customers the way we would like to be treated ourselves."

One thing we all know is: If the business can keep its key customers, it stands a fair chance of survival. Don't worry too much about the competition at this stage. According to Heiman and Sanchez (1998),[2] one of the best and surest ways to lose business is to concentrate on the competition rather than the customer. Concentrating on the competition allows the competition to set the rules of the game, highlights your weaknesses not your strengths, invites price wars, makes you look unimaginative, and above all deflects attention from the customer's concerns.

Skill Set of Your Senior People

The second critical issue that must be addressed in the short term is the skill-set evaluation of your existing management team followed by that of all the staff. Any organization stands or falls by the skill and commitment of the people it employs. It is quite possible that some of the current managers are not up to the job you will now expect of them. It is also a fact that during the first critical period of getting beyond SENIC you will have to manage with the people that are there. There is no time for the introduction of new managers. Let the existing ones show and perhaps even prove and surprise you that they are up to the new demands. If not, you will just have to support them literally and figuratively speaking until more drastic changes can be made. Decide on the organization structure that the business needs to achieve your objectives but keep it to yourself until you know that you have the right candidates for the right positions. In the interim, work on a transition structure where sitting managers can prove their worth.

You might not feel too comfortable initially in evaluating your long-serving employees: this is an area where you can easily find outside expertise for a well-defined project assignment. Get your employees tested by a reputable consultant and evaluate the results with the consultant. Relate your own experiences with all respective employees to the test results. Then you will have to give feedback to the individual employees. The last bit is the difficult one, because you will have to do that all by yourself. After all, you are the owner and general manager. Be compassionate, fair, but straightforward. It is not easy to tell your production manager of ten years standing, for example, that he is no longer the right person for the current job. One way of doing that is to get him to admit that the job has grown beyond him. Most people are realistic enough to know what their own limitations are. The long and short of it is, when you are not happy with him, he cannot be happy in his job because you are continually on his back. Make sure, though, that the examples of underperformance are real and factual. It's a real dud if you revert to statements like, "I can't put my finger on it but I believe that you are prone to making errors," or "Mr. X and Mr. Y have told me that you slipped up badly by doing ABC." Get the facts and examples and then confront.

Critical Functions

Closely associated with the skill-set evaluation is the critical function analysis. Although all the functions in a business are important, some are more important than others in maintaining day-to-day operating capability.

A simple example will illustrate this point: If an account clerk is sick for a few days, it's tough on his colleagues and perhaps you won't get a report or two. But if the sick one is a warehouse employee who operates a very specialized forklift truck for which she attended a course and had to pass a government test to obtain a license, you won't be dispatching goods in a hurry!

Thus, critical functions have nothing to do with seniority or management levels. They have everything to do with the mundane, day-to-day, essential operations. They require specialized knowledge that cannot be gained easily and are critical to your daily process.

Determine where these functions are, and then verify that more than one person is capable of fulfilling them. If in-house or outside training is required, start it as soon as practicable. Not only is this essential for your business, but employees will benefit from gaining additional skills. And I have yet to come across an employee who did not enjoy training. So it's also good for morale.

Delegate

Learn to delegate and what it means to delegate. Don't forget that your SENIC employees have been used to avoiding real responsibility, just claiming the credit for successes. That was the consequence of your own management style; now this has to change. So start easy and let them feel that you support them, but that authority goes with the responsibility. Make them aware of the fact that getting your opinion on an issue is not the same as getting an order from the boss. Get them used to preparing a proposal, verbal or written, then give them the authority to implement. Mentor continuously. At this stage you must be as convincing as a missionary bringing the employees a new religion, namely, "Given the authority, you are responsible for the result." If some of your inner- and outer-circle employees keep on playing the "moi?" game, tell them that these games are no longer acceptable. If they persist, you know whom to replace when the time comes. Remember, the SENIC scene is not for the faint hearted and you, the entrepreneur of days-gone-by, are not in the popularity stakes.

Create some distance between yourself and your management team. Being an owner/general manager is a lonely business, but in order to make tough personnel decisions, close relationships can be a real unnecessary complication. Your team has probably respected you for past creativity; now they will have to learn to respect you as someone who is passionate about giving the authority and the responsibility.

Cash Flow Once More

Insist on getting a cash flow forecast weekly or as often as necessary. All you need is a simple statement that charts cash expected in and cash that needs to flow out (see Appendix C for an example). But what is more important, manage the cash flow and make all your senior staff part of it. Getting the cash in should be a priority for all. Spending it is the easy part. If the cash stops coming in, you will not survive even if all the other short-term goals are reached. Remember the remarks made in Chapter 2, Section "Cash Flow, the Engine of Growth" and Chapter 3, Section "Full Order Books but ..." about managing cash flow.

Labor Relations

Another very important short-term goal is to get the labor union or, if there is no union representation, the office and the shop floor,[3] on your side. It is extremely important that they meet with you, see you frequently in their working environment, not your office, and get to know you well. If you have not spent enough time recently with the rank and file, start immediately and show a great deal of interest in anyone's task. Managing is a people's business and there is only one effective way of doing that—being amongst them. Show interest in what they do. Find out how they do their work and seek means to improve their commitment.

Because a lot of initial issues in the office and on the floor revolve around basic pay, overtime rates, accepted rules of behavior, and basic operational procedures, you can often get effective involvement by the union and/or floor by solving some of the inequalities that have crept in during the entrepreneurial years. Try to stay clear of longer-term decisions; in the initial phase, just level the playing field.

Evaluate Systems

Systems will not make or break your transition process. Evaluate them in the light of your current requirements, cut out unnecessary reports, but leave other ones as they are for the time being. It is far too soon to start changing some of the systems that the inner- and outer-circle employees have developed, sometimes without your knowledge. The resources to properly investigate a new system, never mind how bad the present one is, are just not there yet. Don't condemn the existing system until you're ready to receive suggestions on how to improve it.

What you can do is postpone the introduction of a new computer system if the process can still be stopped. Most SENIC organizations have no resources to form effective user teams to match up with the business and systems analysts that the software vendor has thrown at it. More than likely, none of the business analysis reports and system diagrams have been studied by you or the relevant employees, so the proposed new system is a disaster waiting to happen. Also remember that in the end, an effective system must support your activities but it does not create one single customer.

Financial Institutions

It is highly likely that banks or other financial institutions are involved in financing working capital and capital expenditures. Write a short business plan for their eyes and benefit only, and invite them to a formal meeting. Financiers appreciate it if you call them before they hear that the business is going through a tough phase. What's more, it gives them some confidence in realizing that the current, no doubt for them unsatisfactory, situation is being addressed.

It might also be the right time to look at the current financier's competition. Use the short business plan and arrange meetings with some or all of them. One thing's for sure—your current bankers will take note and show renewed interest. Who knows, another financier might provide you with cheaper money for existing requirements and help you with short-term loans to bridge the SENIC phase. It's certainly worth a try.

Some Fire Fighting Is Required

Last but not least, you will also have to put out fires, if and when they require your attention. Try to determine why something happened. If appropriate, get your management team together to investigate. How did it happen, why did it happen, and can you avoid repetition?

Beware of the trap here. Putting out fires is fun and extremely satisfying, as noted. Before you know it, you will have reinstated the existing team of fire fighters and will leave each evening with a satisfied feeling that you have conquered another busy day. You will promise yourself that tomorrow you will start with "the plan," only to be caught again by another fire. The task at hand is to get your managers out of the fire brigade and into the management team. It's a difficult habit to kick but it has to be done.

Short Term Goals in Summary

In summary, my suggestions for short-term goals to beat SENIC are:

1. Keep key customers happy.
2. Determine the skill set of the existing management team and perform a critical function analysis.
3. Introduce proper delegation.

4. Monitor and control the cash flow effectively.
5. Seek the cooperation of the labor union and all personnel.
6. Inform the banks.
7. Evaluate all the current information systems.
8. Put out some fires, with an eye toward eliminating them altogether.
9. Enjoy yourself!

The last point—enjoy yourself—sounds almost silly, but is meant as a very serious suggestion. It's another real life test to see whether you can transform yourself into a business owner cum general manager. After all no one, least of all an entrepreneur, can cope with change if you hate every minute of it. If you can't enjoy at least part of the "change program," you better get help in order to save your business.

Set the Example

A last subject that must be addressed in the context of short-term goals is the subject of your own behavior. Nothing could be more important for the SENIC organization than your day-to-day behavior in all types of situations. Yes, you are still on the stage, and the audience, your staff, is watching your every move. So, for what it's worth, here is my advice again. Try to be organized, cheerful, and optimistic; appear confident; and set examples whenever you can. Show great interest in everyone's task and lead. You are still the organization's behavior reference and as the adage goes, "Nothing so conclusively proves people's ability to lead others as what they do from day to day to lead themselves."

But above all, start practicing your management skills, lead by example, and get as much input from every employee as you can get. They also have to cope with the changes but what's more, they are the ones that will make your success possible.

Take Action for Short-term Goals

So all in all, coping with change amounts to setting your short-term goals and taking the appropriate action. Just keep that in mind and you won't have time to think about the good old days. It's based on the old Chinese riddles on how to climb a mountain or how to eat an elephant: one step and one bite at a time. Prioritize and act and then keep on quoting to yourself and everyone that cares to listen that, "The best is yet to come."

FREE THROWS
- Listen to customers.
- Remember: Survival and then direction, in that order.
- Decide on the short-term goals, prioritize, and act.
- Set the example.

WHERE, WHAT, AND ABOVE ALL, HOW

Effective leadership is putting first things first. Effective management is discipline, carrying it out.

Stephen R. Covey (1932–)

Follow On

When actions related to your short-term goals are well underway and SENIC is kept in check, it's time to seriously consider the basic questions posed in Chapter 2, Section "Decide on What You Want," namely:

- *WHERE* are you now?
- *WHAT* do you want?
- *HOW* can you get there?

Where

Where you are now is certainly influenced by the current SENIC state and your short-term goals, and the actions that have been or are still to be taken. But it's the right time to ask this question because you have discovered that you are not invincible. The true state of affairs needs to be faced. It's a good time to remind yourself of the "attribution bias" notion introduced on page 58. You don't have to admit attribution bias to the wider world; just be honest with yourself. So with the crisis in check, now's the time to ask that awkward question, "What is my business's current condition?" Remember to get as much input as possible, from employees, customers, outsiders, and so forth. Discount the opinion of anyone who readily agrees with your own evaluation. At this stage, you are looking for honest criticisms of your business not compliments, shoulder claps, or "you are doing a wonderful job" type acknowledgements.

That's why I am going to repeat the statement made in Chapter 2, Section "Decide on What You Want": "Why is this input so important? It's of vital importance because future success is only achieved through the people who work for the business and the clients that are served."

The entrepreneurial days are over. It has to be a team effort and the sooner you find out what your team thinks about the business the better. Don't be satisfied with general statements like, "I think we have done rather well." Look for and demand facts. Similar reasoning applies to getting the "truth" out of your clients. It's often easier because clients will point to your shortcomings without undue concern about their own future. Larger client companies will tell you at regular intervals how you shape as a supplier anyway. For those of you in the consumer market it's a bit more difficult. Some consumers do complain, but a lot of them don't complain—they just vote with their feet. Nevertheless, you have to find an objective way to measure customer satisfaction, and nothing beats talking to them and taking complaints seriously.

It Couldn't Happen to You—or Could It?
TIME OUT 4.2
The "9 out of 10" Management Team with the "2 out of 10" Business

To get some sound input from a management team that is reluctant to come forward with an evaluation of the present SENIC situation, I have often used the following technique.

Design a simple questionnaire in which some general characteristics are asked for, such as, identifying problems, leadership, cooperation with colleagues, and so forth. The characteristics themselves are not that important, as you will soon realize. There should be a fair number of them, say about ten or so, to make it look comprehensive and thorough.

Then ask each member of the management team to rate his colleagues and himself on a scale of one to four for each one of the characteristics: "1" being excellent, "2" good, "3" needs improvement, and "4" unacceptable. As you would expect, and as I have proven time and time again, most managers are reluctant to grade their colleagues and themselves "below the bar"—unless there is a real problem with personality clashes within the team that you don't know about! Thus in general you end up with a pretty high overall score for each manager. Don't share the individual scores with them. It's not important.

The next step is to inform them that each obviously thinks he or she is part of a "good to excellent" management team. With this knowledge you see their faces light up! Then comes the cruncher: You now ask the question, "How is it possible that a good to excellent management team presides over a business that barely scores 2 out of 10 in terms of profit, customer complaints, delivery foul ups, and so forth?" Naturally you have to use your own business's shortcomings to make the point.

The ensuing silence is stony, not golden as the song goes, I promise you! That's exactly where you want them. Now enlighten them on the real purpose of the exercise, namely, that the team needs to address the problems the business has—not award each other medals for jobs well done. That can come later. Then, in front of them, destroy the evidence, the completed questionnaires. They have served their purpose.

The management team must come to grips with the fact that with you, they "are the business," and there is a great deal of room for improvement.

What

What is the strategy bit, as you know from Chapter 2, Section "Decide on What You Want." Some important points must be reiterated, namely:

- You are the owner and you are responsible for the strategy.
- No strong vision/mission anymore? Don't be persuaded by anyone to invent one. Just be very good at what you do and let your customers be the mission statement.

- Planning is not strategy setting.
- Commit your strategy to paper.

At this stage, it's the last point that I want to elaborate on, because most entrepreneurs, certainly the ones I have worked with, don't like putting things down on paper.

If you tell people in detail what your plans are, they also know that you failed—if you do. It's much easier to play things close to your chest. Then you can surprise everyone, including yourself. But this is not good enough for developing your SENIC business. Commitment to goals must be strong. By going public, so to speak, you put your reputation on the line. Your enemies might have fun at your expense if you fail, but you will also get help from unexpected sources, namely, your team and perhaps even your customers. And surely the latter is much more important because you want your business to succeed. The vision needs to get "out of your head and into the organization." How else can anyone help you achieve what you want to achieve?

That's why it's also necessary to make the strategy with its objectives as quantifiable and realistic as possible. It's useful to state that you want to have "zero defects," but what do you have at the moment? If your defect rate at present is 34.8 percent, you are probably unrealistic. Seek a considerable improvement but don't set the bar so high that managers give up before they even start.

A statement such as, "Improve company morale," does not really belong in a strategy document. What is it that you are seeking an improvement on, and how do you measure improvement? The most common so-called strategy statements relate to customers. "Be the supplier of choice," or "The customer is number one," or "Our service is the best in the USA, nay the world," are all meaningless statements. Get better ones that mean something to you, your team, and your customers. Again you will say, "Dangerous, because it can be used against us." Nonsense I say. Everything can be used against you, but you are looking for real commitment from your team and an honest approach to customers. There's an Old Dutch surveyor's proverb that states, "Meten is Weten." That means, "Measuring is knowing." Not everything in life is quantifiable, but your strategy statements or objectives should be specific, so avoid general statements and be quantifiable.

How

This is the real tough one, remember. Say you have a strategy objective that reads, "Increase market penetration of product AA by 5 percent." How are you going to achieve this? Again you have plenty of opportunity to fail by making a commitment on paper, but just do it! It focuses the mind on what you plan to do. If you don't know for sure how to achieve it, maybe it shouldn't be an objective. I know that some of you might say, "But that's what has happened to date. I figured it out on the run and I've been pretty successful with it." So here I am again the spoilsport to say, "You are trying to overcome SENIC and get commitment from your team. How can they commit when they don't know what is required of them?"

Yes indeed there are examples of entrepreneurs who grew their companies on "gut feel" and "on the spur of the moment" to giant empires. These were and are very gifted people. However, most of these empires collapsed when the entrepreneur died, and you know why? No one else in the organization was capable of making a single important decision. They were simply not used to it. Is that what you want?

Where, What, and How

These three simple words represent three simple questions that need answering in order to move your business to the next level of activity. The level of formality that you want to achieve in dealing with these questions is up to you. Keep it manageable and don't turn it into a useless paper trail or a document that collects dust on your bookshelf. Make it a living set of documents that you discuss with your team on a regular basis to determine progress. Don't be put off if one or more objectives fail at the first attempt. To fail is one thing, to never have tried another. Reconsider, redefine, rephrase, ask why, and move on. But from now on for every major activity that you undertake ask yourself the three questions and you will force yourself and your team to think through the actions that are required to successfully complete the activity.

The Budget

A last word on the budget is also in order. Have a budget by all means, but don't kill it with detail. Again, it's very useful to know that your canteen bills are going through the roof, but more important to know why sales targets were not met or margins are deteriorating. Just because it's difficult to determine doesn't mean it can't be done. Anything that's easy to collect, like expenditures, can be divided up ten thousand different ways to be analyzed, scrutinized, and criticized. Just find out why the sales targets were not met or market prices are in a downward spiral. Then you are analyzing properly.

A simple budget geared to your business is useful, but *cash flow is king*. Never forget that measuring and projecting cash flow is infinitely more important than having a detailed budget. Accountancy is history; a cashflow forecast is "guestimating" your future.

FREE THROWS
- Figure out where, what, and how.
- Gather genuine internal and external input.

- Don't forget: Strategy is your baby.
- Quantify and measure.
- Declare your objectives.
- Create simple budgets + "best possible" cash-flow forecasts.

PLANS ARE NOT CHISELED IN STONE

In theory, there is no difference between theory and practice. But in practice, there is.

J. L. A. van de Snepscheut (1953–1994)[4]

There it is! Your mission is clear in your head, you have just finished your strategy for next year, set the objectives, put the budget in place, gotten the cash flow forecast system up and running, obtained firm commitments from your own team and major customers—and then slam bang! One of your key customers goes bust! So much for planning. Let's go back to fire fighting please; at least we were good at that.

Why Plan?

Before answering the fire-fighting question let's first of all consider why planning is essential:

Planning is essential—not because what is planned is going to happen, but what is about to happen can be considered against what was planned.

Appropriate action can then be taken. Sound too easy? Of course it's much easier said than done, but that's where planning pays off. First you can consider the negative or sometimes positive impact of "the unexpected," and adjust your income and expenditure predictions. Don't forget your cash-flow forecast. Sound planning should also allow you to consider the Critical Success Factors and keep them at the level that you know you need to stay in business.

Monitor and evaluate. If sales increase dramatically, rethink the plan. Just because your products are very popular doesn't mean that weekend shifts are called for. Are the margins large enough to justify all the overtime, machinery wear and tear, energy costs, maintenance costs, and so forth? You can't sell part of your production as "manufactured on Sunday" for a premium to recoup extra costs. Particularly in high-wage countries overtime rates of "double on Sundays" and a bit less on Saturdays are fairly common. If it doesn't pay you to increase production, don't. Your own business is not about satisfying all requests regardless. It's about making money. Think before you act. That's the discipline of planning coupled to the monitoring of Critical Success Factors.

Plan B

While it is indeed true that plans need to be formalized, it is equally true that under changing circumstances plans must change to keep the ultimate purpose—a satisfied customer—in mind. That's where you should have the edge over your larger competitors. Your channels of internal and external communications are still short, hence you should discover quickly that the market has moved on or that customer demands have changed—that is assuming of course that your customers are not leaving you in droves because of unspoken complaints. That has nothing to do with planning but sits firmly in the realm of dreadful implementation. Under the heading "planning," unforeseen changes in market conditions are the subject.

If your vision is still powerful, look at the plan, discuss with your team, change the plan and implement. If not, ask yourself: Is my vision strong enough to sustain this type of setback or is it a make believe one copied from something that read so well and sounded really great? Consider this seriously and perhaps start concentrating on "letting your customers be the vision," take action, and change the plan! Please do not confuse these planned changes with producing twenty "what-if" scenarios. The latter is almost too easy with modern spreadsheet technology, but a total waste of time for a small- to medium-sized organization. Spend more time on monitoring what actually happens (customers and cash flow remember!) and adjust the plans and budgets accordingly.

Fire Fighting?

Now let's consider the return-to-fire-fighting question. The answer is: certainly not. I do not compare swift-planned action that needs to be taken in order to adjust to market conditions, supplier price increases, or any other unforeseen circumstances with fire fighting. The very essence of fire fighting in business implies action without a plan.[5] So even if you do have to take some quick ad hoc actions, your passion for the plan should be able to get you back on track pretty quickly. If, for example, a key customer complains about the dimensional tolerances of your latest delivery of widgets being way above the agreed norm, you have a problem that needs to be addressed. Address it! Why have your own quality checks failed? What caused the discrepancy? Are machines, tools, or both at fault, or perhaps a simple operator error? Now remakes are to be made in a hurry, checked properly, and so forth. Perhaps a bit of fire fighting is required but plan changes probably not.

In general one of the golden rules is: things you can't control, don't even try. It's a common complaint in the Western World that time and again deliveries do not arrive punctually because of horrendous traffic congestion. Can you control traffic congestion? You can discuss it, bemoan it, curse it, but in the end the answer is "no." So plan your way around it. The answer might be simple, or more than often somewhat more involved, but be creative. Put on your entrepreneurial hat and find a solution. If you find a way to improve your delivery statistics with that major client, before one of your competitors does, guess where the business is going to go? They don't produce and distribute those delivery statistics for suppliers for nothing.

At all times, fire fighting should be kept to an absolute minimum because in essence it is nonproductive, probably suppresses some major or persistent problem in your organization, and often hides the true cost of your operation by adding expenditure that was not considered initially.

Planning Horizon

Your adopted planning horizon should vary somewhat with the industry, but the "good old days" of five-year plans that were revised once a year in an elaborate planning cycle that started in September and finished in January (it was claimed anyway) are long since history.

For most SENIC businesses a planning horizon of one year is probably long enough. In that case it would mean that you look at your overall plan at least once a quarter, add a quarter to the horizon, and adjust where necessary. That's called a rolling projection, and it gives a better grip on changing circumstances. If major changes occur, of course it's necessary to review immediately. All this planning, making projections, budgeting, and cash-flow forecasting creates a considerable amount of work, so it's terribly important to keep it as simple as possible but nevertheless give it your and your team's full attention. It's easy to let this slip and delegate it to the financial controller without much interest from your side. Don't let that happen. If you lose interest in the plan, your team will lose interest, and before you know it, it will be an exercise that your financial whiz does without any real life input. The only leftover of the whole plan will be a meaningless budget.

If you think the system is too complex for your organization and too labor intensive, change the system. The very basic planning tools are still the cash flow forecast and your Critical Success Factors. For example, if one of your CSFs is the production output per direct labor hour, make sure that's reported correctly. If it slips, investigate. So again, good CSFs will indicate that you are leaving the rails and "going cross country." But in conclusion, the most important thing to remember about planning is that you are doing it to react in time to changing circumstances and to achieve your longer term strategy.

FREE THROWS

- Plan. It's essential. Not because what is planned is going to happen, but because what is about to happen can be considered against what was planned.
- Devise plan B if required.
- KISS.
- Create rolling projections and cash-flow forecasts.

GET YOUR SYSTEMS TO SUPPORT YOUR BUSINESS

Make everything as simple as possible, but not simpler.
Albert Einstein (1879–1955)

It's a pretty obvious statement, "get your systems to support your business," isn't it? Yes it's one of those that sound too simple and the result should be simple, all right, but the sting lies in the definition of the detail. As stated before,[6] there's probably a software package out there for just about any type of business on the planet—and that's the problem! The choice of software systems in the marketplace is horrendous, and if you are not particularly versed in business systems, and most of you aren't, you are a target-rich environment for consultants and software vendors, and not necessarily in that order. Before you can say, "All I wanted was a simple spreadsheet," you are up to your neck in feasibility studies, process diagrams, business analysts, hardware upgrades, and software choices. And you know who the main culprit of all of that is? Yes, you. If you don't define what you actually require, you will get something different.

Requirements

In the jargon, your requirements are referred to as *functional specifications*. But, never mind what you call them. It is obviously important to define what you want something or anything to do. You have done this quite naturally with the main elements of your business. So start applying the skills that brought you where you are now to your systems as well. Do you just want a good invoicing system coupled to a debtor's ledger with some basic control on purchases? Or do you need a full inventory-control system linked to a production and delivery system? A good starting point is to consider your current systems. What do they actually do for you? What would you like them to do? Is it possible to get that out of the current system? If not, is there any other way you can get that information with 80/20 in mind?

Often, the growing business is dearly lacking in planning, whether it is production planning, delivery planning, purchase planning, or all three. First of all try and plan off line so to speak in order to find out how to plan. Develop a system that suits your organization. Sometimes that works for quite a few years until you are ready for the "real thing." If you let loose initially with a full planning system without considering continuous-input requirements, you are just asking for trouble.

Far too often, everyone claims to know what they want but if asked to write it down or draw a diagram the effort falters. If you can define precisely what you need, you are already well past the half-way mark in getting to a system that supports your business. The emphasis here is on *precisely*!

Changes in Systems

If you do decide to change or upgrade some of your systems, make sure that your team is closely involved and totally committed. You must use their knowledge and address their concerns. Make them part of the process, think through all the variables, like the limitations and the advantages, the additional input requirements, the special cases that are not so special like goods returned, and the training of personnel. Often a change in system, dictates a change in work practices. Make sure your staff is ready for that. Employees do get used to a particular way of working, never mind how flawed, and any change is seen as that famous elephant that needs to be eaten. As one of my managers during SENIC times once commented, "There's some serious work coming my way." That he had been fire fighting the weekly delivery schedules for the last three years, juggling two cell phones and a fixed line, sending e-mails for the short pauses in-between rings, didn't seem to concern him. He was used to that. The planning system that was proposed at this point was new and to him meant a change in work practices. And that could only mean more work.

One Way Traffic

Many years ago while I was still working for a multinational that shall remain nameless, I learned a valuable lesson. As a newly appointed junior manager, I was informed by my boss that weekly activity reports by fax were required by some sort of staff department at head office located on another continent. As it so happened, this fax was due two days after I started. Not knowing what to report, I asked one of my fellow managers, who said, "Oh that's simple; just write, 'Due to limited time in function there is nothing to report.'" The week after that I was still feeling a bit uncertain so I asked my colleague again, who said, "Just write, 'See previous week's report." Apparently he had been doing this for over a year with never a complaint, query, or other form of feedback. What went up never came down, not even as a tacit reminder as to content required.

Information that is fed into some sort of system that appears to serve no purpose will deteriorate quickly. Creativity will prevail where correctness is demanded. Thus, if you want your systems to support your business, make sure that information flows up as well as down. Discuss information with your team, draw conclusions, take action if required, and monitor again. There's nothing wrong with sharing all business information with your team. How can you expect them to be committed when you say to them during a meeting, holding last month's confidential variance report at reading distance, for your eyes only, "The results for last month were well below what I had anticipated. I want everyone to pull up their socks and stop messing about." You have to be more specific. They are your team, and they deserve to know what it is they have to improve on. What's more, they must be queried on the actual results themselves.

The System around the System

As important as the system itself is the system around the system. By that I mean the work practices, procedures, and instructions that surround that wonderful invention generally referred to as *the system*. Let's refer to those practices, procedures, and instructions as the *methodology*.

Your methodology must also support your system. Let's use an example as an illustration. In many a small company accounts are kept centrally. If not properly controlled, this often leads to a horrendous amount of extra effort as the accounting person, "the central body," tries to gain information from various sources as to the correctness of, for example, a purchase or an invoice. Missing delivery dockets, checking whether deliveries were actually made, differences between purchase orders and supplier invoices—you name it, the poor accounting person has to deal with it. This is not a very effective methodology. It is much more efficient to delegate purchase control to your staff with a strict system of approval. Hold staff members responsible for getting the documentation together and submitting to the account person. The one who incurs the expense is responsible for initiating and checking the paperwork and matching the latter to the physical goods received. The accounts person checks for completeness of documentation and the correct signatures and can proceed with final approval for payment. This type of methodology is critical to support your system and hence your business.

It's All in the Detail

Some of you might think, "How boring. I am running a business and have no time for that sort of detail." Take my advice, spend some time developing the system around the system with your staff and you won't regret it. Otherwise, before you know it, serious costs are incurred with no benefit at all. In my many years with SENIC businesses I have seen seriously wrong invoices or "forgotten to invoice" non-invoices,[7] considerable overcharges on purchases, suspect purchase invoices based on bulk deliveries that were way out of tune with operating demands, and even phantom employees on the company's payroll. Not to speak of the many scams surrounding those "foolproof" punch clock systems that feed directly into the salary payment system. The clock records correctly and the link to the payroll is solid as a rock, but the system around the system is rotten to the core. Don't get paranoid, but realize that systems need to be checked continually in order to keep everyone honest. One of the reasons I have discovered quite a few scams is by "wandering about" in the office and on the factory floor at random times during the day or night.

Naturally it's important, nay critical, that you, yes you in particular, are seen to be complying with any system you introduce. If you don't comply, you leave the door wide open for everyone to try "his luck" with bucking the system. As ever, your motto should be, lead by example.

The system around the system is also another important reason why Critical Success Factors need to be monitored. If ratios related to these CSFs get out of hand, something must be changing. Find out what it is. It's often the "human touch" that is massaging the system with intent to beat it and in the process reduce your bottom line!

It Couldn't Happen to You—or Could It?
TIME OUT 4.3
Bucking the System around the System

Number one scam. One of the many scams I've come across in my career involved a night-shift manager and his two supervisors, the "three musketeers" as they were known after the discovery of their deception, I might add. The night shift ran from 10 P.M. until 6 am every weekday in a twenty-four hour factory environment divided into three shifts with about 60 employees per shift.

The three musketeers would all clock in on time, but one of them would leave within an hour or so to do "other things." The remaining two would cover for the absent one by acting like he was around but not available. As the factory premises were quite extensive, that wasn't too difficult. By the way, most of the workers probably didn't even miss the supervision, but that's another story. The absent musketeer wouldn't even bother showing his face at 6 am to clock out. One of the others would do that for him.

As the senior management for that particular facility ran a tight ship from 9 A.M. until 5.30 P.M., they had never even seen nor experienced a night shift. The scam was discovered when guess who, the new general manager, took an interest in what happened in a twenty-four-hour period.

So, you say, ah that would never happen in a small company like mine! So here it is, scam *number 2*. Again a production environment with a total of fourteen employees: eight for the day shift and six for the evening shift. The six employees of the evening shift had the task of "clearing" the factory of the day's production. The product had to cure for a certain length of time before it was divided into smaller bespoke units. The evening shift started at 3:00 P.M. An agreement was in place that this shift had to clear the factory regardless of the hours worked, as production the day after could not even start until the day's work was removed to the stock yard. Initially this particular entrepreneur had worked out that it should take between eight and ten hours, depending on how the product was divided up. This "work standard" was set on the basis of some observations during a couple of initial shifts when the factory was commissioned.

What materialized was that the evening shift had the assigned work—cutting, lifting, loading, and moving—fine tuned and frequently finished within a six- to seven-hour period. In turn, each one of the six stayed behind, read the paper and no doubt drank some coffee, for another two to three hours to clock all of them out "officially" at the time he left. This had been going on for over a year before it was discovered by—guess who?

Now you say, good heavens, this would never happen in a very large company. Bring on scam *number 3*, played out in a major division of a multinational. One of the junior engineers, let's call him AWOL, was doing a part-time MBA at the local business school. He found out that he could finish his MBA in two years instead of the regulation three by taking some of the courses during the daytime. We are talking roughly about a commitment of two to three mornings a week for about a year.

The office environment is a large open plan set-up, official background "noise" to dampen the real noise, thick carpets to dampen both presumably, and with those shoulder-high office partitions that allowed you to see heads floating past, heads that would say "morning" to you when you were looking up—something most people did repeatedly because as we all know peripheral vision is much more acute than "straight on."

On the mornings that the selected courses were run, AWOL would come into the office at the regular time, open his briefcase on top of his side desk, hang his jacket over his chair, scatter a few drawings and papers on his desk, and say loudly enough to be heard by at least three or four of his neighbors while not addressing anyone in particular, "I am going to sort this out for once and for all." Then he disappeared. When someone else would ask, "Where is AWOL?" two or three people would volunteer and say, "He is probably in design to sort things out." Design was two floors down in another open-plan maze.

This scam was never discovered but was a "public secret" amongst his closest colleagues! One of which was, guess who? Yes, it was I, before I had the power to deal with such miscreants.

By the way, department heads were positioned along the windows in individual offices well protected from all "that noise" and the hustle and bustle of, dare one say it, the real work.

FREE THROWS
- Accurately define what you want.
- Prepare for changes by getting support.
- Remember: What goes up should come down.
- Don't forget the "system" that feeds the system.
- Lead by example.
- Monitor your Critical Success Factors.

TEAM PLAY IS THE KEY AND COMMITMENT IS THE REWARD

Vision without action is a daydream. Action without vision is a nightmare.

Japanese Proverb

Implementing the Strategy

When your strategy is clear to you, short-term goals are being pursued, your initial evaluation is complete, and the opinions of your "SENIC beating" team have been heard and where appropriate incorporated, you need to set the main course, grasp the rudder firmly, and start the business of recovery in earnest. In other words, now is the time to stop talking about everything you need to do. Start implementing the longer-term action plans and get going on the critical process of operating your SENIC business as a team. It's the team that will now decide whether you are going to be successful or not, and you, as the leader of the team, must guide them through the difficulties of implementing your strategy.

In general, nothing in business is more difficult than to implement correctly what has been formulated as a strategy for a business. Mintzberg (1994), in his book *The Rise and Fall of Strategic Planning*, expresses it as follows when he discusses strategy setting and implementation:

> But all of this may well be wrongheaded, based on a false diagnosis of the problem. It may also reflect who has done that diagnosis: the thinkers, whether senior managers or central planners or the consultants who advise them, people who may have used their "outright dominance" not only to create the problem in the first place but then to attribute the blame for it. Seeing themselves "atop" that metaphorical hierarchy, they point the finger at everyone else, "down below." "If only you dumbbells had appreciated our brilliant strategies, all would be well." But the clever dumbbells might well respond: "If you are so smart, why didn't you formulate strategies that we dumbbells could implement? You knew who we are: why didn't you factor our incompetences into your thinking?"
>
> In other words, *every failure of implementation is, by definition, also a failure of formulation.*
>
> But in our view, this does not get it right either, because it still assumes the traditional dichotomy: that a failure to think it through at the center could be corrected by even better thinking at that center–even more comprehensive and rational thought. This may be asking too much of brains that cannot even handle just plain formulation. In our view, therefore, most often the real blame has to be laid, neither on formulation nor on implementation, but on *the very separation of the two*. It is the disassociation of thinking from acting that lies closer to the root of the problem.[8]

No doubt you will say that the previous quote appears to address much larger organizations. True, but think of it this way: read "entrepreneur" for the "strategy setters," and "management team" for "down below or clever dumbbells," and the portrayed situation in this quote clicks into place for SENIC companies. In fact, the statement is equally valid for you, your company, and the transition period you are going through. Your strategy needs to be absorbed by your team. Just thinking and proclaiming that "your brilliant" strategy is not being grasped by your SENIC organization is indeed the separation of formulation and implementation. That's where the team aspect needs to be recognized by you and developed strongly. But as you, the entrepreneur, are both the formulator and the "chief implementer" of the SENIC beating strategy, there's *no* excuse for the disassociation of formulation and implementation at all! Recognize the dual role and apply the same willpower to this phase of your company's development as you did during the early entrepreneurial years and your chances for success must surely increase considerably.

Passion and Consistency

Nevertheless, a lot of good plans fall at the first hurdle because it takes much more than good intentions to achieve what needs to be done. This is where you must be seen to be consistent and you must stick to the chosen course, unless there are very good reasons to deviate off course. If you want to get from A to B, it doesn't always matter that you stray somewhat or take a while longer, as long as you get there. If you end up at C, you better damned well know why and take appropriate action if required. The luck of some entrepreneurs who appear to succeed in spite of themselves tends not to be associated with the SENIC period. That much should be very clear by now. Entrepreneurs for SENIC companies have to make their own luck. It is hard work and requires a lot of commitment, but of a different type to the start-up phase. The present phase requires an overdose of management! That means the goals must be clear and concise, but above all the implementation must be effective. Fortunately, it is not rocket science either. Generally speaking, most managers, given the same information, will come very close to the same conclusions. So remember, in the end it all revolves around the sound implementation of an agreed strategy by your team. You can no longer go it alone; you need the help of your team, and for that you need to develop your management skills.

Effective Management

Quite a few entrepreneurs will find this particularly challenging. Why is that? Because during the SENIC period the real differences between entrepreneurial and managerial styles can no longer be disguised by enthusiasm, commitment, and hard work but really pop up and come to the surface. Some entrepreneurs, in order to overcome their own management deficiency might even be tempted to involve consultants. Don't! Remember the basic fact associated with almost all management consultants—many have never managed anything in their lives. So letting them loose in a situation that requires management as a first and implementation as a close second is not really going to help. *You* have to manage, *you* have to implement, *you* have to form and mold the team, you and you alone! If you have real difficulty adjusting to this new management role and implementing the strategy with your team, get some help—but on your own terms. There are interim managers who can assist you for medium periods, six months to a year, to get things moving, weed out the weak links in your organization, and strengthen the team where it needs strengthening. I have done quite a few assignments like that but always on a full-time basis. I am not a great believer in the "If it's Tuesday, it must be Trouble Widget, Inc."

It Couldn't Happen to You—or Could It?
TIME OUT 4.4
Oh, For the Easy Life

A contracting company was owned by two brothers, one of them the dominant one, a pretty intense fellow but the driving force, the other one a more happy-go-lucky character who was good at his job but also knew how to enjoy himself. Endless rows took place at regular intervals about the most ridiculous and often insignificant issues. It was always me trying to reconcile and, if possible, settle the disputes.

When I arrived early one Sunday morning at the office, I noticed that the two brothers were there as well. Fortunately there was no one else there. Mr. Driving Force just grunted at me when I greeted him in passing his office, and Mr. Happy Go Lucky in the next office was slumped behind his desk with his hands covering his face. I walked in and asked him what had happened. He told me that he and his brother just had a major row on a minor contractual slip up, but he ended his tale by looking sadly at me and imploring, "And all I want is an easy life."

Before I knew it I said to him, "Let me know when you find it and I'll come and join you." We looked at each other, realized what had just been said and roared with laughter. Mr. Driving Force came in and asked what was so funny. So when we told him he saw the funny side as well, burst out laughing, and promised he would come and join us as well.

---

consultancy approach in which consultants come in on a regular but disjointed basis.

Implement Action Plans

Translate your vision into an achievable strategy and a feasible plan of action. Make absolutely sure this happens. Communicate this to your management team and the organization at every conceivable opportunity. Because, if your team misunderstands "your" vision and "your" strategy, then action plans are doomed, as you will soon discover. With the management team, divide the plans into workable bites and if possible have a plan B when all goes amiss.

Most of the implementation phase must consist of *how* questions. How are we going about the introduction of a basic planning system, how are we going to reduce the overhead by ten percent while maintaining our service record, and so forth. If one of the employees makes a suggestion, ask him, "How will it fit into the plan, how are we going to implement it, and how does it affect other activities?" By asking these questions you make your employees realize that you are seriously considering their suggestions but are looking at the overall picture to stay on the chosen course.

Japanese Logic

Perhaps an old, well-known Japanese management method might help you to accomplish some of your action plans. In some large Japanese organizations, big ideas generated by the top of the organization are fed into the bottom echelon. If the idea takes root, the top echelon then actively pushes the idea up the ladder by encouraging discussions and acting like the idea came from the "floor." If the idea survives the various layers of management it is in effect vetted and just about the whole organization is committed by the time it "officially" reaches the top. The idea is owned by the organization and not seen as another top-down directive. It takes longer than a dictatorial decree, but enthusiasm in implementation is almost guaranteed.

You can implement this in your own organization as well. A simple example will show how. Let's say that you are looking for a more effective layout of your workshop. Innocently ask a number of employees, "I often think that we are not making optimum use of the working space. By moving A to B and X to Y we surely should decrease handling?" Then mumble something incoherent and move on. Let them mull on the idea. Next time you ask, "How would you reorganize the layout of the workshop if you could start from scratch?" Put a zip on your mouth and let them think about it. So you work on them all the time. It takes longer, but what's important is that it makes employees think. It makes them feel part of the team, but above all it should get their commitment and that's what you're really after.

Seek Cooperation and Commitment

This is the second major time period to be a missionary in your organization. First you had to convince yourself and your inner circle that your idea for a start-up was sound and now you have to continually preach to the team about the method and changes you want implemented, so explain "the why" and seek cooperation and commitment. Align the structure with the strategy. Make sure that every employee understands the chosen plan and foster a climate of dialogue and suggestions. Remember, the employees who do the work must implement the strategy, and therefore it is vital that they believe in it, live it, and breathe it. Be a fair judge of who is on board and who is not. All the stuff about inner, outer and expand-contract employees[9] needs to be brought back to the very simple and basic question, who is capable of doing what job? Involve your management team. It's hard for a manager to work with someone she feels is incapable even if he is your favorite employee because he is "fun to be with." Don't give a manager the excuse to say to you, "How can you blame that on me? Mr. Rising Star is totally incapable; I told you so some time ago." Let her manage and take the responsibility with the authority, if you please! That's what it's all about. And if you feel strongly that the manager herself is the weak link, based on facts remember, you know what to do. You might have to make some hard management decisions, but in the end you cannot allow your business to be held back by employees, never mind how loyal they have been to you in the past, who at this stage of your company's development really should be "left behind." There are many ways to repay loyalty, but keeping someone in a position that's grown well beyond her is not one of them.

The Focused, Creative Team

Management is first and foremost a "people's business." Hence, don't be obsessed by control. An obsession with control leads to risk aversion, which means that real creative ideas, well focused on the vision and strategy, are not considered, and some truly great changes are not even contemplated because they are, by their very nature, unpredictable and as such are beyond formal planning. Mintzberg (1994) calls this the "fallacy of formalization." People, not systems, produce innovation, so always be open to suggestions and ideas. Obviously these ideas and suggestions need to be focused on the strategy. Just remember, you don't have to be a genius yourself all the time; you must harness the collective knowledge that exists in your SENIC business, break it open, and teach employees that sharing ideas and suggestions with others is both productive and rewarding. The team must become more powerful than the individual players. This requires commitment by all and guidance by you. If you have done a good job in "selling and merchandising" the course of action, the chances are well above average that you will get that commitment from your organization.

The Visionary Team

During the early years, the entrepreneur, alas unknown to himself, has created a culture of dependence and conformity that tends to obstruct the questioning and complex learning required for innovative action by employees.[10] Now, this culture has to be amended to shift the emphasis from yourself to the organization. In other words, you should be trying to build a visionary organization that no longer relies on you, the leader with "mere vision."

Collins and Porras (1994) explained this difference as follows:

> Imagine you met a remarkable person who could look at the sun or stars at any time of day or night and state the exact time and date: "It's April 23, 1401, 2:36 A.M. and 12 seconds." This person would be an amazing time teller, and we'd probably revere that person for the ability to tell time. But wouldn't that person be even more amazing, if, instead of telling time, he or she built a clock that could tell time forever, even after he or she was dead and gone?
>
> Having a great idea or being a charismatic visionary leader is "time telling": building a business that can prosper far beyond the presence of any single leader and through multiple product life cycles is "clock building." The builders of visionary businesses tend to be clock builders, not time tellers. They concentrate primarily on building an organization—building

a ticking clock—rather than on hitting a market just right with a visionary product.[11]

It is critical, therefore, that the difference between your single-minded entrepreneurial approach, that got your SENIC business where it is, and the visionary approach, that must lead your evolving business out of its first organizational crisis, is developed. Initially, this development always revolves around responsibility, authority, and, not to be forgotten, active listening. The team approach is the only way to move from mere vision to a visionary organization.

FREE THROWS
- Agree on the strategy.
- Concentrate on the details of the implementation.
- Align structure with strategy regardless of past loyalties.
- Always concentrate on how you are going to achieve.
- Remember: The team is bigger than the individual members.
- It must become the team's strategy, so involve them.
- Focused creativity and visionary organization building.

A FAMILY BUSINESS MUST BE AN EFFECTIVE TEAM AS WELL

Family firms are frequently more riven with intrigue and visceral hatreds than a medieval court—and for similar reasons. Substitute the founder for a medieval monarch, and the professional managers for courtiers, add in a pair of rivalrous heirs with jealous wives and scheming cousins, and you have the perfect recipe for a Shakespearean drama.

The Economist[12]

Entrepreneur Take Heed

It has been said already that by the time a business reaches SENIC status, the family of the entrepreneur has started to take a keen interest. Let me remind you of the Irish expression, "Where there's a will, there's a relative." There could already be any number of family members employed in the business. You, the owner, might want to share your good fortune with some other members of the family, and in the back of your mind you might even be thinking of who will carry on the family name in the business. Although these issues should be addressed sooner rather than later, they appear, in general, to get little attention until there is a major family crisis. Most of these crises arise because the rules for family involvement have never been set. Particularly during SENIC, your mind is not really on family intrigue or involvement, but just be aware of the consequences of totally ignoring these potentially fatal problems and start incorporating the family into your "business thinking."

Unstructured Family Involvement

As soon as the family gets involved in the business in an unstructured manner, there is the danger that rational decision making is no longer possible and emotional issues take over. This invariably leads to conflicts with, in particular, non-family senior staff. They find it difficult to understand irrational behavior and decision making by the family that, in their mind, inflicts long-term damage on the SENIC business.

In my own experience, as a non-family general manager, most of the SENIC businesses I was involved in had major difficulties at one time or other with one or more family members employed in the business. Some examples that come to mind are:

- Family member employees that did not have clearly defined roles.
- Family member employees that got salaries way beyond realistic market levels.
- Off-payroll payments to family member employees in order to supplement their salaries, well known to all employees and therefore the more damaging for it.
- Non-compliance with the business norms because after all "we are family," particularly practiced and visible in the misuse of expenditure accounts and the allocation of perks.
- Hiring family members without consulting current management.
- Non-performance or misbehavior of family members that went unpunished.
- Rivalries between siblings.
- Intervention by spouses.
- Unspoken animosity between family members.

Therefore, if there is one subject for a "family business in the making" that must be addressed, it is a policy for the involvement of the family in the business. Unfortunately, in my personal experience, there has never been such a policy. This has precipitated disrupting and sometimes critical conflicts between the business and family interests. The ongoing conflict between "family socialism and business capitalism" is very real indeed.

Here's a somewhat uncomplicated anecdote to illustrate how family socialism can be separated from business capitalism:

> As a business owner the father realized that his son was not what one would call a model employee. In fact, some would say that the son could be considered to be totally useless and unsuited to the business. At long last the father decided to do something about this unfortunate situation and called his son to his office. He spoke to him as follows: "Son, as your boss I have very bad news for you. You are fired. Now as your father, what can I do for you?"

Easily said, but not easily done—but then no one said that dealing with the business and your family was easy. Nevertheless family issues need to be addressed in the context of your SENIC beating strategy.

It Couldn't Happen to You—or Could It?
TIME OUT 4.5
Family Socialism in Action

It was not an easy case to start off with. The organization had been going through quite a few changes, a nice variety of management consultants, and numerous expand-contract supervisors without much improvement. The entrepreneur, let's call him Arthur, had been actively involved himself on a number of occasions in the last few years, but never for any length of time.

His previous choice of a general manager had proven to be an intelligent but lazy individual who could not stand up to Arthur and just clocked time. My involvement started with a long lecture by Arthur about the fantastic organization he once used to have, about ten years before, and it was up to me to make sure this situation was copied forthwith. Fortunately, the product of the business was relatively straightforward and of the commodity variety. The company operated at a loss, but the competition was not fantastic either. There was a chance, anyway.

Most of the employees, about two hundred, were as cynical as one could imagine after ten years of consultants, bad management, and needless changes. The inner-circle managers were in well above their head, groggy with outside advice but fervently loyal to Arthur. Bring on myself, the fifth general manager in ten years. It took me awhile to get employees and management to realize that I took this assignment seriously. Arthur did not make it easy for me and we had countless arguments on relatively minor issues when he "touched base" at very irregular intervals.

Suddenly, after about twelve months, he summoned me cheerfully to his residence and informed me that after ten years of mutual silence, he had made up with his brother, Bart, who was now to join me as "joint managing director." He waved aside my passionate objections, and Bart joined the SENIC scene.

Apparently, Bart used to work for Arthur in the past and many of the inner-circle managers still knew him. After some prodding they told me that he was not very effective, nor very popular, and that his management style was somewhere to the right of Genghis Khan.

I observed the situation for awhile, had a couple of major rows with Bart, and decided to approach Arthur again. Arthur tried to pacify me but insisted that I work with Bart.

The organization, inevitably, sank back into passive inaction and blind obedience.

Family Norms and Values

Conflicts cannot be avoided, but when they arise they can be dealt with more effectively if the family itself decides, within their own norms and values, how to deal with these conflicts in the context of the business.

Hence, a good start can be made by discussing and formulating what could be called "the Family Norms and Values." These are the rules and regulations that you, the entrepreneur, and your family members are bound by when dealing with company issues.

In a recent special report on family businesses in *The Economist*, the contention is made that if the following three major decisions are made properly, the family business has a better chance of surviving:

1. Make-up of the board.
2. The terms on which family members can join the firm.
3. Creation of a strategy, for the business and the family.[13]

This special report discussed much larger family-owned firms, but the points made are just as valid for the SENIC business. The earlier these major decisions are implemented the better the chance that family crises related to the business are dealt with in an acceptable manner according to the agreed framework. Some elaboration of these three major decisions is required to explain why they are so important. These include:

- Industry-wise non-executive directors who have no relation with the owner-manager or his family can contribute significantly in giving sound strategic and operational advice. Steer clear of close friends. It's advice and guidance for your business that you are after, not personal friendship. Forget the "fun to be with" factor and look for added value.
- Also, it is absolutely essential to define the role of family members who are employed in the SENIC business in accordance with normal organizational principles and requirements. To put it bluntly, Is there a job? What is the purpose of the job? What are the objectives of the job? Who does the family member report to? What is the pay rate for the job? It is extremely demotivating for existing management and staff to see a son, daughter, nephew, or niece of the entrepreneur introduced at a level where they are clearly not capable.[14]
- And as for the strategy, I have for some time been expounding on the merits of having one for the business, thus one for the family is a logical extension. Remember though, KISS—Keep It Simple Stupid!

A Family Strategy

Thus, the missing link at this stage is a Family Strategy. This strategy combined with the norms and values can address issues to be considered when families and business overlap:

- Family-ownership succession.
- Family-management succession.

- Recruitment and retention of non-family management.
- Balancing the family and business priorities.
- Developing the leadership skills of the next generation.
- Determining the suitability of the next generation for the business.
- Handling misconduct by family employees.
- Dealing with conflicting visions within the family.
- The involvement of in-laws.
- Estate planning.
- Preserving wealth.
- An exit strategy if so desired (like an MBO or MBI[15]).

These are all essential issues that need to be addressed to help concentrate on the ultimate mission of the SENIC firm: overcoming the crisis and performing consistently.

FREE THROWS
- Remember: Your family is important but so is your business.
- Keep in mind that family socialism can be expressed in various ways and needn't always include a guaranteed job.
- Decide on family norms and values.
- Create a strategy for the interface of family and business.

CUSTOMER LOYALTY IS THE GOAL AND SUSTAINABLE GROWTH IS THE PRIZE

Opportunities multiply as they are seized.

Sun Tzu (c. 544–496 B.C.)

And so, after having explained to you in some detail what needs to happen in order to overcome SENIC, we are back once again with the customer or the Big C, as I call it. That's where it started and that's where it must continue in ever-increasing passion, and if you really want to grow, in ever-increasing numbers.

Internal Problems Are Just That

One of the reasons I keep on hammering the customer angle is the really quite amazing fact that a large number of management books don't even consider customers as an integral part of management. It's planning, procedures, and internal processes that have the limelight, as if these internal essentials alone would cure your business problems. Your real problems and challenges are still out there because, believe me, your customers are not in the least bit interested in your internal problems. They are simply interested in your products or services in relation to their own wants and needs.

Once you engage your customers, you must forget all those "domestic hassles." Don't bore them with the details of your "restructuring process and the introduction of that new enterprise resource planning system" to explain why their deliveries were postponed again, or worse, blame it on some mix-up between your organization and your subcontracted hauler. They are bad excuses and my standard reply in situations like that is to grab a handkerchief, start some serious sniveling, and say, "That's nothing, now do you want to hear my problems?" Internal problems are just that and of no concern to anyone else and certainly not your customers. I've had some real good times with suppliers and more often than I care to remember with accountants, lawyers, and consultants. To a series of basic, sometimes crucial typos, their "professional" excuse was invariably, "We are short of office staff and the work was not done by my regular assistant." The well-known saying, "the buck stops here," should be adjusted for lame excuses by these folks to, "The buck stops at my assistant. I'm only the boss." So throw up your hands, admit the slip-up, and correct it as soon as possible. It's awkward but much more appreciated.

"We don't look for excuses but will seek a solution" should be a useful slogan for your SENIC-beating team. Imprint this on the minds of your team and your whole organization. If you don't spend your time looking for excuses, you can spend more time looking for solutions. Get the embarrassing bit out of the way, find out where the internal problem is, and give the customer feedback without running down one of your managers or a department. It's still your business. Take that responsibility and teach that responsibility to your senior staff as well. I've often said to customers, "I don't know what happened but I will find out and phone you back in a couple of hours." Then I did whether I knew the answer or not. Be reliable and punctual and don't hide behind internal problems.

It's the Business, Not You

A very difficult transition must also take place. You, in particular, must start to let customers know that they are doing business with your organization and not with you personally. That is difficult, because you were and probably to a large extent still are the business. How you do that cannot be prescribed, but what you can do is put the right people in your organization forward at every opportunity. Just work on that and you will create an atmosphere of "us, the business" rather than "me, the entrepreneur." We all would think it's ridiculous to phone Bill Gates if we have a problem with one of his products. That, of course, is an extreme example. Nevertheless, in your SENIC business start practicing the art of putting the organization first and yourself second when it comes to customers. Customer loyalty needs to be attached to the business first and yourself second. That includes your star inner-circle salespeople, who often act like they personally are holding the whole business together. I've frequently said to paranoid entrepreneurs, who were held to ransom by salary demands of good salespeople, "Is that what you think of your own business?"

Of course there are consequences when an effective employee leaves your organization, but slowly and surely you need to accept that your business can be and probably is already larger than each individual employee. After the resignation of, for example, John, one of your key salespeople, quick visits to major customers with the "new face" and even possibly yourself often confirm that they liked dealing with John all right, but they are much more interested in your product offerings, possible discounts, and your service. If John does walk off with some of your customers, you have a problem. Obviously customer loyalty was directed at John and not your business. Find out why, correct the situation, and never let it happen again! Building your business's reputation to foster customer loyalty has to become the goal without delay for "post SENIC."

Not Customers, Your Customers

That brings us again to the questions, Who are your customers? Have you defined them well enough, and do you know them well enough so you can react swiftly to their changing demands? Find out why these customers are still with you and what sort of growth potential they have. Can you piggyback on their success or have they reached their limit? Research similar customer companies and find out who their suppliers are. Pay particular attention to aggressive companies that are about your size—you can grow with them! Foster relationships with your key customers that are difficult to break, for example, integrate logistics systems, keeping stock for them, and then deliver on demand, increase the service level that "integrates you" in their system, and so forth. The possibilities are endless, and you, the entrepreneur, with your team, will have to find the ones that are unique to your environment. Be very wary of outside advice regarding these customer relationships and particularly by consultants. Their advice with regard to these matters is often based on what they have gleaned from your competitors or the major players in your branch, and that's not necessarily what you want. You want some degree of innovation, not duplication. Duplication is often why price wars squeeze out the smaller players. Even small innovations, never mind where in your whole process—purchasing, production, sales, and so forth—can give you the edge, for a while anyway. It's all about differentiation and breaking open existing "taken for granted" products by introducing what is sometimes a minor addition or variation.

Active Listening

Listen, listen, and listen again to your customers. Most of us find it difficult to listen. We are so full of our own ideas and perhaps our own agendas that we forget that the answer might lie with active listening to what our customers are saying. Active listening is the process of really concentrating on what someone is saying without preempting or starting to think of what you are going to say yourself. Count to ten slowly and silently and keep repeating to yourself, "I'm not going to interrupt." You can also encourage the other party by nodding agreement and asking a follow-on question or just staying silent. Your silence is often interpreted as "more information needs to be given," and that is what you often get. It all sounds difficult enough but practice frequently and you will soon get the hang of it.

A close relation of active listening is not putting enough distance between your own ideas or preferences and those of customers. This is particularly difficult to understand by entrepreneurs that have fallen in love with their own products. There's nothing wrong with liking your own products, but you want to make a living as well. A friend of mine, employed as a merchandising director in the furniture trade, once told me, "It took me some time to cop on but my taste was totally different from the average punter that visited our shops. The more hideous I thought something was, the more units of that particular item were sold. So I changed my buying behavior and mainly bought things that I disliked intensely. Sales went ballistic." Somewhat exaggerated no doubt, but it makes the point: Find out what your customers want, not what you like yourself, something you know already! Sometimes a small modification for a production item, suggested by a customer that you might think is ridiculous, will make one of your products that much more desirable for all your customers.

There's another advantage to developing your active listening skills. This is where your young business should have the edge over much larger competitors. In large companies the "change route" is so fraught with real and political obstacles that some sales representatives in these organizations don't even bother to try. Their loss is your opportunity. By listening and adjusting to your customers' requests you might just have the edge on reaction time and that certainly builds customer loyalty.

Growth Must Mean Focus First

Size almost invariably means that a certain amount of specialization is called for. All these unusual "one off" requests made for loyal customers will now have to be considered in the light of your growth and your organization's capabilities. Find out what your popular product lines are and examine their growth potential first. Look at the pricing of these products, the costs associated with them, and optimize their contribution. That's pretty tedious management work, but optimization of contribution lies at the heart of sustainable growth.

Not that long ago I was associated with a SENIC business that had two main lines. Let's call the remaining line *specials*. The percentage of total sales for these 3 lines was about 70, 25 and 5, respectively. Unfortunately, the entrepreneur and his inner-circle team were spending more than 50 percent of their time on the specials at the expense of the main business. It was fun you see, reminiscing and reliving the start-up years. Many hours were spent perfecting that one-off unit for Mr. "Client of the First Hour," who visited almost daily to discuss progress and frequently introduced a few more modifications that he had thought of while inspecting the latest

It Couldn't Happen to You—or Could It?
TIME OUT 4.6
Lateral Thinking in Action

It's a story that was told to me and my fellow "business studies part timers" in the 1980s, by a professor of marketing, as an example of lateral thinking or as consultants would call it nowadays, "thinking outside the box." The person in question would probably call it plain common sense!

It was purported to be true. I have heard it a few times since and have used it myself on appropriate occasions.

The product, let's call it WOW, was a cleaning agent in the form of a powder that came in a long tubular container, about nine inches long, two-and-a-half inches in diameter, and with six small, quarter-inch holes punched in the top lid. The product was dispensed by holding this dispenser upside down and shaking it well. WOW was extremely popular, but of late its sales figures were showing definite signs of the downward sloping part of the well-known product life-cycle curve. The marketing and sales department of the WOW manufacturing company had been experimenting with all sorts of gimmicks. Strong lemon flavor was added, then color was tried, then various colors with various flavors, and so forth. All these were, for WOW, fairly expensive additions that achieved absolutely nothing. In marketing terms, the various varieties simply replaced the sales of the basic product but did not increase total sales of WOW. The sales curve kept edging in the wrong direction. It was what could be called a very "well done" and mature product.

One day an exhaustive but so far fruitless session on how to increase sales, where a lot of "out of the box" thinking had already been done, was interrupted by the arrival of the working lunch. First things first and "brains" require nourishment too. Naturally, it was difficult for the participants to get back "into the box" to eat lunch like mere mortals, but the topic of the casual conversation was similar, namely, how to increase the sales of WOW. One of the waitresses serving the lunch shyly, almost hesitantly said, "I can tell you how to sell more WOW." You could hear a pin drop in that room filled with the best marketing brains that particular company could muster and aided by some pretty expensive strategy consultants. Together, they had probably been thinking so far away from the box that they had lost sight of it altogether! Then with a trembling and soft voice the waitress continued, "put another hole in the top."

Needless to say, sales of WOW went up by 16.67 percent within a very short time and the life cycle of WOW was extended by a few more years.

prototype—all in all good wholesome riveting stuff but unfortunately not very profitable. The two main lines, far from trouble free I might add, were left to the resources of the lesser mortals. That was and still is a very dangerous habit unless the two main lines had been running so smoothly that they could have been considered the "milk cows" for this particular special or "new star." Alas for this company this was not the case. Focus on the two main lines was required, but attention to specials was given.

Of course we all know that sustained growth must ultimately come from a nice mix of current and new product offerings, but first things first. Create a solid base and generate some regular cash flow before your organization ventures into other related pastures. Focus and perfect your current lines before looking at additions.

The Black Box

Sustainable growth is the formal way of saying that you are prepared and can cater to plenty more customers. That's the bottom line. In practice it means that you will have to examine all your internal processes and streamline them as much as possible.

For your customers your overall internal process is the "black box." Most customers don't really care what happens in this black box as long as their orders come out with the required goods and at the required time. So the black box is your concern and yours only.

The point has been made on a number of occasions that the difference between the entrepreneurial and the directional phase is organization. In general, working harder will not work any longer, because it's about working smarter. That's where the study of process flow comes into its own. What you need to do is study your process flows and improve them so in theoretical and ultimately practical terms, they cost less, involve fewer employees, take less time, but nevertheless can cope with a load increase. Before you grab the phone to charter a couple of consultants consider the following. You and your team will have to do the hard work anyway so you might as well get on with it and only seek help when you know exactly what you want.[16] Depending on how complex your internal processes are, coming to grips with them is not an easy matter, but like everything else in life if you do it "one slice at a time" you can do it. After all, you and your team should know the current situation better than anyone else, and in order to improve you must first know the current situation in detail.

What you are looking for first and foremost is a system that does not depend any longer on individual know-how. The system needs to be transparent for everyone and easily transferable to additional employees. No longer is it sufficient to have the inventory clerk, one of your trusted sidekicks, decide where to keep stock. After all, he has been with you a long time and knows every corner of the stock room. No, every item of stock needs to be tied to a location for everyone to "see"—no more creativity, not at that level anyway. It's like the saying, "Creative accountants go to jail." Lots of the processes in your business should be void of any creativity but follow a certain set routine. However, don't dismiss creativity for standard processes altogether. Sometimes a shy office clerk might suggest an improvement in a procedure that could save you thousands. But you need to have a procedure first before you can improve on it.

Customers and Internal Flows

It's perfectly true that customers in general would not be interested in your internal flows. However, there are exceptions. If your product is a sensitive or critical one, or related to the food or pharmaceutical industries, your internal processes are more than likely subject to "audits" from your customers. If you supply products for those industries, you are probably used to a certain amount of process control and would find it relatively easy to increase the level of this control in order to satisfy your own and your client's requirements. But beware; it's a bit like those ISO systems. It's your business that needs to get beyond SENIC, not the client's or the ISO certification body, for that matter. Just by satisfying some type of external audit does not mean to say that you are efficient yourself. I did a stint at one of the many suppliers for a major "blue chip" car manufacturer. This company had landed the contract of its dream with the major car manufacturer—great margin and an almost-guaranteed take for five and perhaps even ten years. The parts this organization supplied were only a minor subset in the overall scheme of things, but the specifications were rigorous and the paperwork horrendous. The organization was well thought of by the car manufacturer, but was in SENIC in a real bad way. Its own processes were atrocious and its own internal reject percentage for the parts in question was well beyond 40 percent—result: key customer very happy but organization doing all the things I have described during SENIC times and well on the way to becoming another statistic. So just because you are satisfying an outside requirement doesn't mean you are effective. You are effective when you make an acceptable profit margin and your customers are happy.

Without a customer there is no business. But some customers help you to an early grave! Make sure you know what the consequences are in doing business with very large customers and judge whether your organization is ready for it. If your own internal processes are "bedded down" and working well, the chances are you are ready to play in the bigger league. That's sustainable growth.

Cash Flow

At this stage, it almost goes without saying that cash flow[17] is a vital part of a survival but also a growth strategy. Monitor it carefully and make absolutely sure that while your sales are really getting up steam, your cash flow is not running out of it! Sustainable growth also means controlling your cash flow and not operating beyond the realms of what is financially possible.

FREE THROWS
- Keep internal problems internal.
- Promote your business, not yourself.
- Don't sell what you like, but what your customers want.
- Focus before you spread yourself.

- Get your internal systems functioning well.
- Ask: Are you ready for some customers?

CONSOLIDATE AND FOLLOW THROUGH

Success usually comes to those who are too busy to be looking for it.
Henry David Thoreau (1817–1862)

Know Your Own Business

This is a bit of a funny one to discuss, most of you might think. Of course you know your business. But do you really? Really knowing your business is being familiar with every aspect of it. And that in turn means that you know where the real strengths and real weaknesses of your business lie. Fortunately you are no longer alone, so "knowing the business" is of course a team exercise. Decide on what are the most important aspects of your business and "walk and talk" through the processes. For example, discuss the current process of sales order to delivery. How does an inquiry become an order, who can decide to "enter into a commitment to deliver," who can determine where and when to deliver, and who knows whether the item is available in stock or needs to be ordered or made, and so on.

In a recent assignment, I was associated with a SENIC business that supplied a number of processed products. There was nothing novel about these products, but the business had grown considerably by adopting the "we never turn a customer away" approach. After a few years, without too much thought, the business started introducing a second production shift to cope with the demand. The orders kept on coming, also from customers that competitors had shied away from, until the yearly figures came out for the year SENIC was reached. Market prices for the products had dropped considerably during that particular year, and the wage bill, made up of overtime and the second shift, was staggering. Within one year the company went from sound profitability to small loss, quite an unexpected shock for the entrepreneur but a classic SENIC case for me. After some fast calculations it was decided to reduce the workforce, only make a certain quantity of products in a given time, and profitability would return forthwith. Unfortunately all the assumptions to arrive at this recovery scenario were based on the wrong assumptions, as was discovered pretty soon. Certain actions in the factory were thought to take Y hours but in fact took 1.5Y. Tasks that used to be executed with XX employees required XX+X because part of the factory was inaccessible due to high stock levels, additional machinery, and so forth. Clients that should have been charged extra for quite substantial product alterations were charged the standard rate, and so on and so forth.

To make a long story short, the SENIC business no longer operated at the initial cost variables. Processes had been amended without control.

Effectiveness was sacrificed for "let's get it out of the door, regardless of cost, to satisfy the customer." To top it all, the products were being sold as "off the shelf stock items" while an individual customer-project approach was required. Nevertheless, the inner circle claimed to know the business like the back of their hands. The point to remember is: if you can't describe it or measure it—find out and describe and measure it. There are no short cuts for this, only many different ways to do this in practice. Don't make it more complex than it is, but if it is complex don't avoid it either. And why is that? The long and short of it is, it's impossible to consolidate something that slips through your fingers like a wet bar of soap in the shower. You can play with it and if you're lucky you might even catch it without slipping on the wet floor, stumble onto the solution so to speak, but the chances are you won't, and you will land on your you know what. You are trying to consolidate and that requires knowing what is happening in detail.

Don't be tempted to throw a software solution at it either. Computer systems can make life a lot easier, but if you don't know your own processes you better find out first before you make the situation even worse! Do use the collective knowledge of your business and concentrate on the value-adding parts of the business. Of course you can, for example, computerize your employee records to incorporate all the wonderful things associated with a "human resources best practices" system. Every human resources professional will argue that these processes "add value" too. I'm certainly not disagreeing, but if you are bleeding badly at the order entry, inventory, and delivery system, you can make up your own mind what adds more value for your organization. If a computerized planning system sounds like "just the ticket" to control your production process, make sure you understand that process fully before you introduce it. In the realm of production, logistics, or resource planning there are more failures recorded in SENIC businesses than all other business systems combined, as far as I am concerned anyway. That's not because these systems are inherently flawed, but because your own "system" is not a system as yet and needs to be much better investigated and defined.

First things first, not dissimilar to "get the short-term goals moving before you start on the longer-term plan," get your processes defined and described before you even think of software solutions. Your own team and the organization is the key to unlocking what your current processes are. Outsiders can help, but rely first and foremost on your own staff.

Group Think

Just a word of warning on the phenomenon of "group think."[18] Group think is the process in which every member of the group reinforces, for whatever reason, what someone suggests to the extent that a dissenting voice is no longer allowed at all. In other words, a different opinion is not tolerated and is seen as "treason" to the course everyone has "agreed" to follow. Therefore, listen carefully to any nonconforming voice, and if everyone too readily agrees with your own opinion, remember you are still the "overpowering" entrepreneur; change it and see what happens. Particularly during the process of getting to know the intimate details of your business there should be a lot of disagreement as to what these processes really are. On many occasions in the past, I've heard various people describe the ostensibly same process in many different ways. Sometimes the only conclusion you could draw was that there was no process to speak of. But at least everyone was thinking about what they thought the process was. That's what you want to achieve. Disagreement often leads to a better understanding of a process, so avoid early "easy" acceptances by the group. Think about any possible way to make them justify their opinion and clarify easily reached points of view with regards to present situations.

Optimize and Formalize It

Having found out what the present actual processes really consist of, the next step is to optimize them. Every process and associated procedures can be improved. Depending on your own priorities and of course resources, concentrate on the value-adding processes before you think of the nice-to-have processes. This is where your knowledge of the Critical Success Factors of your own business must start to pay off. Optimizing a process can be done in many ways but the most time-consuming method is also the most foolproof one that achieves long-term results. This method is based on changing one thing at a time, measuring whether the desired improvement has been achieved, and then moving on to the next improvement until the whole process is optimized. Sounds complicated? Not really, it just takes time, control, and patience.

Naturally if there are some blatantly wrong practices in a particular routine, you must eliminate these immediately. You don't have to spend weeks in investigating the "tightening up" of the procedure for buying office equipment. Nevertheless nowadays, anything associated with computers, like paper or print cartridges, needs a simple procedure and some associated controls to make sure that someone is not using your paper to run their small independent print shop during office hours. Decide who can order, where, and how, and then control the expenditure.

It has often surprised me how little control there was in many a SENIC organization that I have been associated with for purchases of raw materials. Stock control on bulk raw materials that are being transformed into your finished products is not that easy to control accurately without a fully fledged inventory system. But you can achieve 90 percent accuracy by simpler means. For example, if you know how much of bulk raw material X, including some wastage, is used to produce Y, start with an inventory of stock. Then at regular intervals deduct what should have been consumed by your own manufacturing and what has been added by the bulk raw materials supplier. Then take stock again. At least you "control" the situation regularly and in the process might learn something about actual usage in your factory. Concentrate on the main ingredients for your production process, but don't forget the high cost small items. Don't start counting the paper clips and elastic bands if you haven't got control of your major purchasing items and of course your finished product inventory. Please, let common sense prevail at all times.

Plan It

Planning is often started with great enthusiasm to conquer SENIC and just as often quietly forgotten because, "Our business doesn't lend itself to planning." The main reasons for that "early surrender" scenario are threefold:

- *Planning shows up all your own internal weaknesses.* All the stretch in your own SENIC organization has been reached some time ago. Working smarter is required, not working harder. Often when planning is started, a lot of things get even worse before they get better because you are trying to superimpose a system on what was some considerable degree of disorganization. Stick with the planning and spend time discussing with your team how to get out of certain undesirable situations without throwing the baby out with the bath water. But insist that planning is here to stay, continually seek ways to improve the planning process, and make sure the team understands the plan.
- *Your customers don't "seem to want to cooperate."* But how can you expect your customers to cooperate with a system that more than likely is to their apparent disadvantage? Apparent because once the planning system is better developed, you can stick better to your promises than ever before. They were probably used to a system that required frequent phone calls, promises made and broken, deadlines missed and reset, begging and threats, just "not" in time deliveries, and partial deliveries "to keep them going." Give them time to start relying on your scheduling of deliveries with 95 percent certainty of "on time" and they will change their tune. That will take awhile, but if you don't start now you will never get out of SENIC! Remember, in one or two years some of your new customers won't know any better than that you always produce and deliver according to sensibly agreed schedules.
- *It's difficult to change entrenched practices.* That's a difficult one, but entirely internal, fortunately. How you solve that dilemma depends on how entrenched the old practices are and who is trying to convince you that it "will never work." Depending on the circumstances and the person involved, you can vary your answers to these "early giver uppers" from "If you can't do it I will find someone who can" to "Please give it a chance before we decide that it doesn't work, because there is no way back." Whether you like it or not, people don't like change because it's a venture into the unknown. It's much easier to fall back into old habits, never mind how unproductive these were. Often planning seems even more, and certainly more difficult, work than firefighting. That is why the team has to believe in itself. Tweak the planning system by all

means, but don't let them give up. Work it by means of paper, wall boards, spreadsheets, or whatever other means are available to you. Just find the system that works for you and your organization and don't allow your team to look back. Improve, perhaps by only one step at a time, but all the time.

It Couldn't Happen to You—or Could It?
TIME OUT 4.7
Customers and Planning, the Twain Shall Meet Eventually!

It happened a few years ago, the country, the industry, and the company—let's call it NOCLUE Ltd.—don't really matter. NOCLUE had been pretty successful by adopting but also living up to the slogan, "We never turn a customer away." When SENIC was reached, about eight years after initial start-up, I was asked by the entrepreneur to sort things out.

There is flexibility in every system, and the flexibility in NOCLUE's case was its staff. The commitment of staff to work any hour of the day and night, including Saturdays and Sundays, made it possible for NOCLUE to receive any potential customer with open arms, which were also the ones that the competition didn't want. In other words, at NOCLUE the staff was the ultimate "stretchable resource," but at considerable cost. But like all stretch, if you overstretch you lose all stretch, and that's what had happened at NOCLUE—no more stretch, only staff just barely limping along trying to cope with an ever-increasing workload and yet more frustrated customers. Customers were being serviced on the basis of "who shoutest the loudest gets the fastest." On top of all that, over the last year or so, prices for NOCLUE's products had decreased by about 20 percent—all in all a very worrisome combination that had resulted in a substantial loss for the previous year.

After a couple of weeks, the short-term goals of NOCLUE were formulated. They were solutions designed to help in figuring out who the customers were, forecasting cash flow, and planning for production.

Having decided on the internal responsibilities, the "new" management team was set to work on coming to grips with planning while the sales staff was learning to say "no" to the unfortunate organizations that were not on the new customer list.

Information of what had to be produced was hidden in the various departments of NOCLUE. Quite a few intensive sessions later we thought that we had a fairly complete picture of what NOCLUE was committed to in the next few months. Now for the detail! A weekly planning cycle was decided upon as being the most realistic to start of with.

The first day of the "new plan" had hardly begun when some regular customers had already called in with changes in their not-yet-fulfilled" orders. Some wanted their stuff earlier, others were not ready to receive theirs, and still others decided to amend their original specifications. In other words, "the plan" was being amended almost every couple of hours. With new orders, customers were being told that production was fully committed for the next fourteen days, but they would be "the first in two weeks time." Some customers had difficulties with that, others threatened to put their business elsewhere, while still others almost went ballistic. This type of service was not expected from NOCLUE at all. After all, NOCLUE had been at their beck and call twenty-four hours a day seven days a week! Wisely enough, the entrepreneur owner had decided to take some "well earned leave" and entrust customer relations to his team and myself.

After a day of extreme spread-sheet gymnastics, no one really knew any more what the original plan looked like, and production was chaotic. There were so many changes that we had lost count. Not surprisingly, this carried on unabated for a couple of days. To achieve a planned situation after years of "free for all and may the loudest customer win" is not a week's work, but may take some time, I had assured the team after encouraging them to weather the storm and stick with it. After all, planning was here to stay to get out of a fairly precarious situation and we could not "service" the world with our limited production capacity.

A couple of weeks later, some significant improvement had been achieved but we were still struggling to get on top of things. One of the overworked planners remarked dryly to me, "It sounded like such a great idea this planning lark. But some of our customers don't seem to understand our planning."

Get Commitments from Your Customers

Part of the process of growing up as an organization is to get commitments from your customers for longer time periods. In most industries, it is possible to discuss longer-term arrangements with customers if it's beneficial to both parties. Longer-term arrangements mean that you can move the operating horizon of your business forward by a significant time period. With operating horizon, I mean the time frame of guaranteed continuance—guaranteed, as guaranteed nowadays can be of course. That's why you should never become complacent. The emphasis might be shifting from acquisition to "maintenance selling," but the stakes are always the same. Even long-term contracts for the supply of your products to any one of your customers can be broken open without any difficulty if you do not fulfill your part of the bargain. So just stay close to your customers, regardless or whether they are new or have been with you for many years.

As you can imagine, these longer-term arrangements with clients are very helpful to your planning process and, not to forget, your actual cash flow and the cash flow forecast as well. Planning becomes easier if your clients have regular demands that are tied in to your planning cycle. And with regards to regular payments, I don't have to explain that to you at all. It's almost like being on a salary! Just stay alert and recognize early signs of customer irritation.

Longer-term arrangements also have the advantage that you can spend more time investigating your internal processes and optimize them. In manufacturing terms, one speaks of the experience curve, a downward-sloping cost curve as a function of time. That's the sort of momentum you are looking for to achieve longer-term profitability. After all, the downside of long-term contracts is that it's often more difficult to obtain a price increase even if you feel you are entitled to one. As a result, improvements in your bottom line have to come—above all—from your own efficiencies, and lest you have forgotten ...

Inverse Marketing

At this stage of the game, I don't have to hide the topic any more as I did in Chapter 2, Section "Your Customers are the Key to Growth." Efficiencies of your own organization very much involve practicing the "art of inverse marketing." Examine all your purchasing arrangements and if necessary "break them open." With your suppliers, discuss better prices, just-in-time deliveries, better terms, better everything. In view of your own longer-term arrangements with some of your customers, you can probably get better terms from your suppliers if you can offer them a more regular "take off" pattern. Put on the pressure, look for possible second sources for major items, and compare regularly with possible alternatives. But please do remember that, not unlike real marketing, one has to look at the "total package." Reliability, quality, and service come at a price, too. Don't let "to buy cheap" become "to buy twice."

The Human Factor

One word on those marvels of communication, the Internet, intranet, and other potential nets and e-mail. It seems that nowadays, a lot of managers relate their importance and their degree of activity to the number of non-spam e-mails that they get and can answer—cries like, "I was away for one day only and I had to deal with eighty-seven e-mails in my inbox. It took me the better part of this morning to deal with them."

Such laments are supposed to indicate how vitally important this particular manager is to the running of the business. Don't be fooled! Modern methods of communication are marvelous, and I for one could not do without them. However, the chances of being distracted by all the "noise" created by these communication media is horrendous and, in my opinion, one of the main reasons why managers get diverted from real people management and real-life business issues, like customers, while being ever so busy and often disorganized.

Here is my advice: It is not bad practice to first of all pay attention to the human factor in your business by wandering about at length or alternatively visiting clients with the sales force. It is remarkable how much you can still learn from your business by being here, there, and everywhere. After you have spent a considerable amount of time in this activity, absorbing real business life so to speak, have a look at your e-mail. If something was really urgent, the person would have phoned you.[19]

Follow Through

As in golf, having started the swing you might as well follow through and finish the shot as best you can. After all, there should be "a light at the end of the tunnel" coming up soon unless, as was relayed to me once by a dry-witted upstate New York CEO, whose subsidiary in Europe I was guiding through SENIC, "The light at the end of the tunnel is an express train coming towards you at 140 miles an hour."

FREE THROWS
- Know your business.
- Beware of group think.
- Optimize, formulize, and plan.
- Get customer commitment.
- Practice inverse marketing.
- Remember: It's the human factor that really counts.
- Recognize the difference between daylight and artificial light in tunnel vision!

NOTES

1. Drucker, P. F., *Management, Tasks, Responsibilities, Practices* (New York: HarperCollins, 1985).

2. Heiman, S. E. and Sanchez, D., *The New Strategic Selling* (Boston: Warner Books, 1998).

3. "Office" and the "shop floor" mean the people who actually do the work, either on the shop floor, the warehouse, internal sales, administration, and so forth.

4. This quote has also been attributed to Yogi Berra (1925–).

5. That's where I must apologize to real-life fire fighters, the employees of the many fire brigades around the world. They most certainly plan how to tackle a blaze and train for such an event regularly. Then they just have to do it on the occasion and mistakes can be deadly!

6. Chapter 3, Section "Systems that Dictate Your Business Needs."

7. If you charge too much you'll hear all right, but if you undercharge you never will.

8. Mintzberg, H., *The Rise and fall of Strategic Planning* (England: Prentice-Hall Europe, 1994), p. 284–285.

9. See Chapter 2, Section "Your Staff Is a Close Second."

10. Stacy, R., *Managing Chaos: Dynamic Business Strategies in an Unpredictable World* (London: Kogan Page, 1992).

11. Collins, J. C. and Porras, J. I., *Built to Last: Successful Habits of Visionary Companies* (New York: Harper Business, 1994).

12. Special Report, "Family Businesses; Passing on the Crown." *The Economist* (November 6, 2004): 2.

13. Special Report, "Family Businesses; Passing on the Crown." *The Economist* (November 6, 2004): 5.

14. The practice of letting family members work elsewhere, with a bit of luck successfully, before considering them for a function in your business is often much more appropriate.

15. MBO: Management Buy Out. MBI: Management Buy In.

16. See Appendix B about employing consultants.

17. Chapter 2, Section "Cash Flow, the Engine of Growth," and Chapter 3, Section "Full Order Books But ..."

18. Janis, I. L. & Mann, L., *Decision Making: A Psychological Analysis of Conflict, Choice and Commitment* (New York: Free Press, 1977).

19. And if they didn't, you better teach them to use the phone for urgent messages!

5

The Ones that Went Before:
Some Successes and Failures

Never interrupt your enemy when he is making a mistake.
Napoleon Bonaparte (1769–1821)

THERE'S ALWAYS A FIRST

Of all the SENIC assignments that I have had, the first one still sticks in my mind like it happened yesterday. Perhaps it's like your first car, long since gone but close your eyes and crank you memory and—boom—it's there in all its nostalgic splendor. By now (2007) it's about twenty-six years ago. The business, SNACK Ltd., was a snack-food processing company that had recently been bought by an ambitious entrepreneur, Nigel, who ran a similar but much larger operation in a neighboring country.

The entrepreneur-about-to-depart of Nigel's first foreign acquisition had timed his final and ultimate sale to perfection, as the business was pretty run down. It was, so to speak, balancing precariously on the very end of the entrepreneurial growth curve. The tired and out-of-date plant was easily recognized by Nigel and his accountants, but operational and managerial problems are seldom discovered during a due-diligence process. Nigel probably thought that he could fix most of them anyway. He appointed the sales manager as managing director and one of the production supervisors was promoted to production manager.

Some major difficulties at SNACK came to the surface quite quickly. The previous entrepreneur, H-ACTIVE, had ruled supreme. Accordingly, even his senior staff was totally unfamiliar with decision making. From production priorities via delivery schedules to client negotiations, the whole organization was like a headless chicken. The two newly promoted managers did not seem to get much respect, either. This was further complicated by dissimilar systems and a fair dose of national pride.

Within months, SNACK had moved to a loss situation. Frequent visits from Nigel, also an H-ACTIVE type, and his senior staff, did not seem to help much. It's difficult to be H-ACTIVE in two places at the same time, particularly if one of them is foreign and you don't speak the language. Eventually, Nigel decided that he should seek outside help.

Unfortunately, Nigel's cousin was a management consultant for one of the larger international practices. He suggested that their local office could provide help on a part-time basis. Before long, a "Tuesday to Thursday" consultant was added to the overhead of the newly acquired foreign subsidiary. This did not seem to help much, but it did provide Nigel with substantial reports, pages of sales analyses and production-output graphs, not to forget the illegible flow diagrams that were purported to show how the systems of both companies could be integrated.

After about two years of continued losses, Nigel had enough and instructed his accountants to sell SNACK.

Nigel had paid top dollar for the acquisition but now he found that the best offer he could get was not even a tenth of the original purchase price. At this stage, I was brought into contact with Nigel. Nigel really had enough of "foreign" operations and wanted out as soon as possible. But he didn't want to take the loss either. He was caught between the proverbial rock and that very hard place.

My brief was quite clear: SNACK had to be brought back to profitability in two years and then would be sold to the highest bidder. After some discussions with the resident consultant and having familiarized myself with his analytical insights and countless recommendations, I told him that I had no further use for his services. Although Nigel was somewhat taken aback by my instant decision, he probably felt that he had little choice after two years of advice.

During the first week at SNACK I demoted the sitting managing director back to sales manager and the production manager back to supervisor; they didn't seem to mind much at all and appeared almost relieved. Then I started interviewing all supervisors and staff. Morale was rock bottom and reception was almost hostile. (Don't forget: After two years of remote control by Nigel and his staff and part-time exposure to an open-ended consultancy presence, SNACK was in "Ostrich Mode.")

Four weeks later I had visited the top fifteen clients with the sales manager. The overall picture was not very flattering. The main complaints were inconsistent quality and unreliable deliveries. Processing equipment was in a bad state of repair and upgrading was out of the question due to the considerable cost involved. When I visited Nigel's own processing plant for the first time, it struck me that it looked similar but in much better condition. So I approached Nigel and asked him if I could set up a little intercompany project group to study whether processing for certain products could not be combined. When this proved feasible I was ready to present Nigel with the plan. It was suggested that SNACK would be tuned down to a sales and distribution business only. The majority of products could be processed at Nigel's plant and all others could be purchased from third-party processors. This would:

1. Keep vital client links in place as SNACK would still have all the actual client contacts.

2. No further investment or maintenance expenditure would be required for the out-of-date processing equipment.
3. The current facilities could be converted to additional warehouse space, and the location of SNACK was ideal for this purpose.

The downside of the plan was the layoff of more than half the current employees. This could be achieved over time as each production line was discontinued, but would involve substantial payouts and a lot of time in the local labor court for me. The conversion of processing facilities to extra warehouse space would require some capital expenditure.

Nigel agreed to implementation. The worst production line at SNACK was stopped and product was sourced from Nigel's own plant. With the usual hiccups, this started to operate well within a couple of months and costs were not far from those predicted. After all, most of the cost parameters were well known, and transport from his plant to SNACK was the only new variable. Over the next nine months, all other processing lines were closed and the product portfolio was sourced entirely from the parent company and outside suppliers. Naturally, we took a good look at the product portfolio as well and rationalized it as much as possible.

In the meantime, I was reorganizing and converting from a processing emphasis to a sales and marketing one. My best appointment was a new quality-control manager who was utterly unmoved by the most persuasive sales arguments, and in a relatively short time created a fantastic rapport with all the major clients. He caused quite a few logistical nightmares by his intransigent stance in setting and maintaining quality, but our standing with clients improved considerably. In addition, he proved himself to be a very capable product developer and made countless suggestions for product variations.

Another important appointment I made was a logistics manager. With deliveries to major clients almost every second day, it was crucial that the flow of goods was maintained at all costs. We adopted the system of the parent company to save time and the new software was up and running within a year. Ninety percent of our transport requirement was outsourced and the only transport we kept were a few delivery vans for logistical emergencies.

The sales manager was shaping up quite well. We strengthened his department by adding two young marketing specialists who were fantastic in dreaming up all types of special promotions. When you have to fight for every inch of retail shelf space with your competitors, it's a very useful capacity to have. With quality at previously unheard of levels and a much better delivery performance, we also enhanced our negotiating position.

At the end of the first year SNACK broke even, discounting the once-off costs associated with the reorientation plan. The following year, SNACK was back in profit and Nigel appeared to have forgotten about selling. As a bonus, the additional volume had increased the efficiency at the parent main plant. I stayed on for an additional six months to assist Nigel in selecting a more permanent successor. Ten years later Nigel sold out completely, as far as I'm aware, to one of the major European food processing companies.

EIGHTY PERCENT OF WORK IS PREPARATION

The business, CONSULT, was a medium-sized consultancy[1] specializing in negotiating cost savings for client companies for all their supplies. This was done in transparent fashion. In other words, the client company itself would negotiate for new supplier contracts with CONSULT orchestrating and directing the whole procedure unknown to the suppliers. All negotiations were carried out strictly by correspondence between a client company CEO and the relevant suppliers.

This was done to upset the often cozy relationships that exist between suppliers and their customers. If you don't believe this is possible, have a talk with an office-supply sales executive and find out how they manage to get top prices from an awful lot of businesses. CONSULT got paid on a "no cure no pay" basis to the tune of a percentage of first-year negotiated and proven savings.

The owners of CONSULT, two very much ACTIVE entrepreneurs, argued vehemently and continuously with each other. This did not seem to distract them at all, because somehow they had built up a very, and I mean very, profitable business. However, growth and, even more so, profitability, had stagnated quite abruptly. Their own efforts to overcome this phenomenon had consisted of hiring more client-acquisition executives. When I started, there were nine of these well-paid gentlemen spread throughout the land. Control of these free-flying or free-waltzing, if you like, executives was minimal. As long as they had a number of appointments every week, the owners of CONSULT appeared to be satisfied.

The first thing I did was to investigate what the current *hit rate* actually was. All concerned were quite surprised to find out that the current rate, based on definite client visits, was about one in eighty. Taking into account that over a hundred telephone calls had to be made, often to as many companies, to secure an appointment with a CEO, the hit rate was even more discouraging. With chances like that, any salesperson would be taken by surprise if she did actually score! Further investigation found that the only marketing tools in use were the yellow pages and information gleaned from the various company registry offices.

In summary, client acquisition was a bit of a hit-or-miss affair and not really based on any marketing premise at all. Clearly, some analysis was needed. Not much historic information was available, so we had to theorize as well. In a number of free-flowing sessions with the owners and the acquisition executives, we agreed on the following parameters:

1. It was critical that the customer company's CEO be our main contact.
2. It was thought that medium-sized companies were the best target market.
3. Companies in industries that had low operating margins would be more interested in possible savings on purchases.
4. The raw material purchases for a company were less interesting than the secondary purchases, such as packaging for the finished product, consumables, stationery, computer supplies, and so forth.

5. The more personnel were involved in secondary purchasing, the better the chance of substantial savings.

Based on these parameters, we started to target companies. The hit rate went up but was still far too high. Then something else struck me. I had noted, during my own acquisition visits, distinct differences in the location of the purchasing manager's office. If his office was close to the executive suites, we appeared to have little chance. If his office was somewhere else in the building, the chances improved dramatically. Was status of the purchasing manager an important criterion? And if so, how could we find out? After all, we had to get an audience with the CEO to sell the concept. Then I remembered the office-supply sales trick, lavishing attention on the receptionist, that ultimate source of all-around company information. So before we even approached a CEO we would find out where the purchasing manager was located relative to the CEO's office and, what's more, who the purchasing manager reported to.

About a year later we had the targeting fine tuned. Our target market consisted of:

1. Medium to large-sized companies. Subsidiaries of multinationals were particularly sound prospects.
2. Industries with relatively modest operating margins.
3. Purchasing management not part of the executive.
4. Stationery and other minor purchases made by different employees, the more the better.
5. Recently appointed CEOs, one to two years, who wanted to impress.
6. CEOs that had a reputation of being hands-on.

The selling pitch had been perfected also, with great emphasis on the fact that savings in purchases fell straight through to the bottom line—no dilution and no additional effort required at all.

The hit rate went up dramatically and approached the one-in-twenty level. Preparatory work increased tremendously, but we reduced the field staff to three acquisition executives. By the time one of these made a first visit to the CEO of a potential client, a large amount of information had already been collected. So the saying, "eighty percent of work is preparation," certainly proved true for this assignment.

NOT FOR THE FAINT HEARTED

Construction is my favorite industry. Every project is a new challenge, deadlines always have to be made, circumstances change, and pressure is the order of the day. It's not surprising that construction is classed in the upper spheres of stressful environments. This particular construction company, CONSTRUC, a relatively small rural player, was no exception.

Started by the father of the owners, it turned into a continuous family struggle after his death. Initially all three brothers were involved, but after

It Couldn't Happen to You—or Could It?
TIME OUT 5.1
Welcome to a SENIC Scene

My introductions to SENIC companies have been as varied as cloudscapes in the sky. I have experienced quite a few from no introduction to elaborate programs. The one described here was particularly memorable.

The company in question employed about one hundred, with fifteen in the office and eighty-five in the factory. The business had been losing money for the last three years, and the banks had been making ugly noises. Most of the talks I had with the owner-manager, type H-ACTIVE, let's call this one Rolf, were held either off-site or after hours on-site.

First day on the job rolls along. I presented myself to the receptionist and asked for Rolf. Rolf duly came and led me to his office. He mumbled something about "having an important meeting off-site, but I was free to use his office" and left me.

I decided to take a walk and see what would happen. My first stop was the sales office. I greeted everyone, introduced myself, and asked who the senior salesperson was. The gentleman in question raised his hand. I walked over to him and asked him if he could spare me some time this morning in Rolf's office. He looked somewhat puzzled but agreed to meet with me. In the conversation it became clear that Rolf had sort of announced my arrival to various people, but not what I was actually going to do. Terms like, "coming to assist," "giving some guidance," "advising us on," and so forth were used by Rolf, but no indication was given as to my actual position.

Not wanting to usurp Rolf's position, I decided to play neutral for the time being. This "being unaware" routine repeated itself a number of times with the other department heads. After a brief tour of the factory, where I got plenty of stares but no challenges to my presence (it must have been my eyes), I decided to call it a day and left.

In the evening I managed to get ahold of Rolf and asked him how he wanted me to proceed. Then the story came out. He did not want help at all. His accountants, who had acted as the go-between and had drawn up the agreement for my services, and the company's bank, had insisted that he employ a general manager in order to get the business back on track. Rolf was of the opinion that he was only suffering a temporary setback and in a couple of months all would be well again. When I asked him what he was going to do in order to achieve this feat, he seemed somewhat taken aback and told me, "Nothing special, the same as always." When I suggested to him that "the same as always" probably led to his current position and something more would probably be required, he asked, "What, then?"

When I told him that I did not know yet, he replied, "And you are supposed to help me."

what must have been a momentous row, one of them set up on his own company not far from the original premises. The two remaining brothers had a peculiar relationship that varied between love and intense hate.

Nevertheless, when I appeared on the scene, this partnership was wobbling but still standing. The oldest brother, Ned, was the real driving force. An exceptional net-worker, he was responsible for most of the acquisitions. His vision was to be one of the top-ten construction companies in the country. The younger brother, Alf, was a very competent builder. He was more involved with the day-to-day operational problems. Most of their projects had been relatively small, rural ones, but Ned had been networking patiently but aggressively for some time in a major nearby city. Suddenly, Ned struck gold and acquired a couple of large projects that represented three times as much value as last year's sales.

Construction is no different from other industries. As long as you are small, you can get away with minimal paper work and record keeping. When you get larger projects, operating without paper trails is no longer possible. There are so many parties involved, from the client representatives to the smallest sub-contractor, that not keeping proper records is akin to signing blank checks. Both Alf and Ned were not really versed in the art of formal project correspondence whereby every query needs a reply unless you want to be hit at the end of the project by all sorts of claims.

Introducing a system of formal project administration was a challenge, but what was even more of a trial and more urgent was to get the people on board and a management structure implemented that could actually do the work. Between Alf, Ned, and a dozen or so excellent foremen, there wasn't much to the organizational setup of CONSTRUC. In quick time, we accomplished a major recruitment drive. This intense campaign yielded some excellent managers for building operations, cost control, and engineering. Using them to select staff, we filled the ranks below as quickly as possible.

Another feature of size was the necessity of a quality system and health-and-safety procedures. Ned had actually assured the new clients during the lengthy negotiations that we were busy implementing both systems and that the relevant certificates were "as good as in the post." So it was up to us to fulfill this contract requirement as soon as possible.

As a management team, we met just about every other day to get to know each other, discuss progress and bottlenecks, and implement some simple policies and procedures gleaned from previous work experiences. These sessions lasted until the early hours of the morning; discussions were often heated but always yielded some sound decisions. It's amazing what a competent and committed group can achieve! We all worked sixteen hour days and ate, slept, and dreamed concrete. They were exciting times; we were building a couple of major structures and a company at the same time.

When you grow at such a pace, cash flow is always a major concern. Particularly the first six months saw some very interesting times. CONSTRUC was not used to dealing with large subcontractors who could actually afford to stop work on your sites if they didn't get paid! Getting progress payments became an obsession with all and the simple one-page cash-flow forecast became the document we all lived by.

How did we get through it? First of all, I am not a great believer in trying to catch up and integrate old with new if it has to happen within a relatively short space of time. My motto in a situation like that is, "Don't catch up—get with it." What I decided with Ned and Alf is that we would create an independent operating unit "CONSTRUC NEW," based in a separate downtown office that had little or nothing to do with the existing rural CONSTRUC setup. (CONSTRUC was still averaging about six to nine small projects at the time.) The only area that I kept centralized was the financial side. CONSTRUC had some very reliable and efficient administration staff. So, I decided to strengthen this department from the bottom up. I delayed the introduction of a much-needed new accounting system to avoid getting bogged down in implementation difficulties while the major financial problem was cash flow. Although this meant that a fair bit of work was carried out off-line, the older staff was totally familiar with the current routines and, with some extra help, coped well.

A year later we started implementing a new operating and accounting system. The market was buoyant and Ned kept on surprising friend and foe with his ability to acquire new projects. By the time I left, CONSTRUC was among the top twenty construction companies in the region, highly profitable, and poised for even more growth.

WHEN A NIGHTMARE TURNS INTO REAL-LIFE MADNESS

John, a second-generation entrepreneur, had inherited a sizable and modestly profitable catering distribution business from his father a few years back. He had obviously decided that the current business was limited in scope and had opted for an expansion into the industrial kitchen installation market.

Unfortunately for him, he was totally unsuited for this new direction. He never really made a profit on installation activities that were subsidized significantly by the distribution business. There was a family non-executive chairman who had insisted that he seek the help of an outsider to get the business back on track.

When I took the helm, the distribution business was still profitable but suffering due to lack of attention. The installation business was losing money. Overall, the business was losing money and the bank was getting impatient.

The non-executive chairman, John, and I agreed that the distribution business needed to be kept at all costs and that we would tune down the installation business to selling up-market kitchen equipment.

Now, about fifty percent of the distribution business relied on a concession from a very large ice cream machine and ice cream mix manufacturer, let's call it ICE Ltd. Margins were not great, but it was steady, reliable, and almost guaranteed income.

One day, John tells me that he has seen a new Japanese ice cream machine in a trade magazine that would cost only about half of what our present machines, obtained from ICE Ltd. cost. He also tells me that he can get ice cream mix for about 70 percent of the current price from an independent dealer. Doesn't that sound great?

I tell him that it sounds great all right, but can we please first concentrate on parts of the business that are broken and leave the unbroken bits alone for a while.

The next day John does not show at the office. The day after he still does not surface and I phone his home. His wife tells me that he has gone to Japan. About a week later John arrives back at the office and tells me triumphantly that he has managed to buy one of these fantastic new Japanese ice machines. He has arranged the airfreight and it will arrive in the next few days.

When I ask him what the plan is, he tells me that he is going into competition with ICE Ltd. and is offering his machine plus the cheaper ice mix to all our customers. Now the reader must be made aware that the products of ICE Ltd. are a household name in the country where this all takes place, so I tell John that I don't think this is a good idea at all. John, the non-executive chairman, and I have another meeting. We tell John in no uncertain terms what we think of his plan and tell him to focus on the present difficulties.

The Japanese ice machine arrives. The next day, John, who suddenly becomes hyperactive, and a complete installation crew are trying to get the machine to work. Instructions are unfortunately only in Japanese. Countless ice creams are produced, tasted, and discarded, the machine gets adjusted, more mix, more ice creams tasted, discarded, and so on and so forth. This goes on for a couple of days. I am furious, the other crews are complaining, and the customers whose kitchen installation work has now been delayed are seeing their announced restaurant opening days not being made and are threatening me with legal action. The long-serving supervisors have to choose between listening to me or John. I have no chance. John is in the grip of an ice-cold demon. He eats, sleeps, and drinks the Japanese ice machine and eventually announces triumphantly that the "quality is now as good as ICE. We now have JOHNICE."

The next chapter in this drama is about to unfold. I get a call from ICE Ltd., who needs to meet with us to talk about trading terms for next season. We duly meet but during this meeting, John tells the ICE Executives that this will be the last time they can dictate terms to us because he is starting nationwide with JOHNICE. The ICE executives stand up and leave and the next day there is a formal letter in the mail informing us that our area distributorship has been terminated forthwith.

Strictly speaking, ICE Ltd. can't take such drastic action, but ICE can afford the lawyers and we can't even afford our own wages. Within twenty-four hours, ICE appoints a new area distributor. This distributor wastes no time and informs all our clients of this change. Clients phone us, we have one week's supply in the warehouse, but then it's over.

In one fell swoop, 50 percent of our distribution sales and profit has been eliminated. John makes gallant attempts to convert some of the clients to JOHNICE, but to no avail. Suddenly John realizes what he has done and he reverts back to masterly inactivity. A week later the bank hears about our escapade with ICE and demands a meeting.

We are now well into the doomsday scenario. The non-executive chairman and I agree that continuation is almost impossible. John disagrees. When we meet with the bank, they listen sympathetically but are nevertheless merciless in their action. They foreclose.

WHO IS THE CUSTOMER ANYWAY?

This subsidiary of an international organization, in a made-to-order production environment, had been the black sheep for some time. While the other subsidiaries, similar in set-up, were doing relatively well, the one in question could not get its act together. The sitting managing director was ineffective, couldn't say "no" to customers, and steered away from production responsibilities. His production manager was seldom seen on the floor, and first-line supervision ran the factory. Integration of the various production activities was a matter of negotiation between supervisors who appeared to spend most of their time on this activity. Needless to say, a profound knowledge of the "moi?" game rules was an integral part of the supervisory skills set.

The major contribution of the N-ACTIVE entrepreneur to this sad state of affairs had been disgust and masterly inactivity. Cultural animosity between head office staff and the subsidiary were a real issue as well. To put it bluntly, the subsidiary was in a sorry state. Amongst a host of other problems, this lack of leadership had led to a situation where production was manipulated by whoever had the most pull at any given moment in time. It was not unknown for sales executives to influence machine operators to get production priorities changed. Also, some of the production supervisors managed to get their favorite customers to the front of the production queue. Even the financial controller had entered the priority game. Needless to say, chaos reigned supreme. Few people knew what was actually being produced and the planners spent most of their time on the phone explaining why certain things had not happened, could not happen, or were possibly going to happen.

When I took over, I soon realized what was happening. Orders that were fulfilled as planned were almost unheard of. Because the factory ran three shifts, every morning was "lucky dip" for production output. Sometimes none of the orders that were planned for a twenty-four-hour period were executed. It was like an invisible hand was steering the production output while in fact everyone with a bit of influence was tugging at the helm. Sales executives, the sales office, and the planning office were constantly on the phone to irate customers wanting to know what had happened to their orders. Dispatch was kept in blissful ignorance and deliveries were difficult to arrange, to say the least.

In situations like this, it is important to get back to basics and ask yourself, who are our clients? After a number of sessions with the sales force, we had a list of clients by volume, contribution, complexity, and delivery requirements. These parameters resulted in a customer list ranked according to their importance to us. Armed with these facts, I called the production planners together—the production manager had resigned and I was in the process of hiring a new one—and told them that the production schedule had to be built around the requirements of the top twenty customers.

In a fairly simple planning system, production slots were reserved for these customers. I then told the production planners that the remaining customers would be treated on a first-come, first-served basis unless I personally agreed to a different priority. According to the principle "Things will have to get worse before they get better," it took a couple of months for everyone to come to grips with this new discipline. At one stage I threatened to take the telephones out of the planning office and fire anyone who dared interfere with planned production. Some of the lesser clients complained bitterly and some even left us, but complaints from our major clients lessened dramatically as their deliveries became much more reliable. After about a year, we found that production volumes had increased also, due to minimal interruptions and less time spend on retooling.

In times of operational difficulty it is as well to remember that, "All customers are equal. But some customers are more equal than others."

FREE THROWS
- Operational problems are never discovered during a take-over bid.
- "More of the same" is not always the best solution.
- Eighty percent of work is preparation.
- It's all about the team.
- Don't catch up—get with it.
- Some customers are more equal than others.
- KISS is never out of date.

NOTE

1. Yes, I must admit it, I have done assignments for consultancies as well. My excuse is the "no cure no pay" bit that made this particular consultancy acceptable to work for, even in my book.

6

Conclusion

Never mind all that; the best is yet to come.

SENIC Motto

It is a well-known fact that very few start-up businesses make it beyond the first year. Couple to this the observation that only one in three family businesses make the transition from one generation to the next, and you can understand that reaching the first revolutionary phase, in whatever time span, is quite an achievement for you, the entrepreneur, and your business. When the business reaches this phase, another challenge presents itself. Your developing organization's predicament, in this book referred to as SENIC (Still Evolving Now In Crisis), is in need of a powerful dose of direction. Direction and control will make further growth of your organization possible and will avoid the fate bestowed on the majority that will disappear, disintegrate or be relegated to the bottom league.

COMMON FAILURES

The common failures of SENIC businesses primarily revolve around inadequate management, lack of customer definition, bad planning in general, and cash-flow planning in particular. All of these shortcomings are coated by a powerful layer of "entrepreneurial ego."

Entrepreneurs tend to have very strong egos. They must have, to start and grow a business, sometimes against all odds, and with loads of blood, sweat, and tears. Unfortunately, this ego, well developed and even reinforced by the time an organization reaches the SENIC state, is also the greatest cause of most SENIC failures. By having brought the organization from its early beginnings to the first organizational crisis, "typical" entrepreneurs really think that no one can tell them anything anymore. After all, they have been successful and always right in the past. Why should that be different now? Alas, at the SENIC stage, this entrepreneurial character trait tends not to pick up the warning signs in the market environment that things are about to change. No notice is taken of potential problems on the horizon, and in some way successful entrepreneurs believe that they are immune to regular market forces. Also, entrepreneurs' "success is my middle name" self-esteem makes it difficult to listen to suggestions from their own personnel, and more often than not it prevents them from recruiting suitable personnel.

DNA OR MANAGEMENT CORE

The first people that have been recruited for the venture are critical to the development of the business, but unfortunately more often than not, the average entrepreneur, will fill his ranks with friends, acquaintances, and family members. It is the most predictable way to increase the chances of failure. Why do entrepreneurial personalities choose family and friends in these early recruitment decisions? They like to be surrounded by admiring "fans," and that is what friends, acquaintances, and family members are. The entrepreneurs, the creators of the venture, are now in grave danger of becoming their destroyers unless the symptoms are recognized and action is taken.

The family, active or not, can become a great liability, and trusted employees, particularly the inner- and outer-circle ones, are probably the wrong DNA—management core—for the future development of a business. It was fun and rewarding to work with them, but now the "nice to have around" aspect needs to be eliminated in favor of the "fit for purpose" principle. Further, singular, as in "entrepreneur," needs to be adapted to plural, as in "team."

TEAM PLAY

The first revolutionary phase requires well-thought-out and robustly implemented direction changes and not more "can do" disorganized chaos. Working smarter not harder must become the credo. What is required is management and probably an overdose to start with. Sound management gives direction, sets the norms and values of the organization, but above all creates commitment. Commitment in turn creates an environment of intrapreneurship for the sudden unexpected leaps forward that every organization needs from time to time. In other words, what is required is to build a visionary organization that can keep on reinventing itself, because it has learned that the collective wisdom of all employees by far exceeds the vision of one man. Strong management is not an ego trip, nor is it about a high-profile general manager. It is all about building a solid business in which marketing and innovation, as a matter of course, are understood by all employees, and the big C gets the attention it deserves while internal processes are optimized "to make it all happen" in the background.

TRANSITION AND CUSTOMERS

The transition from entrepreneurial to directional also means that the business needs to be promoted strongly as "the business" and not a cluster of individuals. Client loyalty needs to be directed towards your business and not the entrepreneur or for that matter your star salespeople. Salespeople have the habit of referring to customers as "their" customers. Make sure that, when all is said and done, that relationship is directed towards the business and not the individual. "Infiltrate" clients at various levels in order to make it more difficult for them to replace you with a competitor. If possible, increase your service level, integrate your logistics, and so forth. But above all determine who your customers are.

CHARACTERISTICS OF SURVIVAL

The businesses that survive appear to have quite a few things in common, namely, they have learned to adopt a more formal approach for customer satisfaction, have developed an effective management team with or without the extended family, but above all have given due consideration to the simple but exceptionally important question, "Who are our customers?" Planning comes naturally to the successful post-SENIC business and cash flow is KING.

SHORT-TERM GOALS AND LONG-TERM VISION

The post-SENIC business has set realistic short-term goals but has also started the slow process of moving the organization from a single-owner-driven vision to a visionary organization. This process could take quite a few years, but if the entrepreneur and his management team get it right, the organization will become truly effective. Marketing and innovation will be an integral part of the business and not just another "flash in the pan" thought out by the entrepreneur, his staff or, even worse, consultants. If there is a lack of a clear vision, "let your customers be the vision" and concentrate on getting your service levels second to none. In time "the vision" will emerge and then it will be much more powerful than some grandiose statement concocted by someone and no doubt liked by all but practiced by none.

FAMILY INVOLVEMENT

There is nothing wrong with wanting to turn your venture into a "family concern." However, make sure that family socialism and business capitalism are separated and that family involvement in the business is regulated by the "family norms and values." Think seriously of instituting a board and get one or more non-executive directors that are not related to you or your family, do not form part of your circle of friends, and are well-experienced industrywise executives. They can provide independent advice and make "groupthink" unthinkable.

CONSULTANTS OF THE MANAGEMENT VARIETY

Be careful with consultants and before you entertain their services take note of the guidelines given in Appendix B. If you need help, hire it, but on a full-time basis on your terms. Don't be tempted by consultants who deal with your organization on a part-time basis unless it's a very specific and well-defined assignment. "If it's Tuesday it must be SENIC Scenes Inc." scenarios are not good enough for your business. Many management consultants, including the ones specializing in strategy setting, have never managed anything in their lives, so don't let them loose in a situation that requires management first, like dealing with the SENIC scene. At best it's going to cost you a lot of money and at worst it's a disaster waiting to happen. Let me remind you of what "the Don" of the consultancy world once said: "Making real decisions in a business is a lot harder than getting paid to advise people what to do."[1]

INVERSE MARKETING

SENIC also requires a sound dosage of inverse marketing. Inverse marketing will make you "lean and mean" on the purchase side and, coupled to good management and an organization "fit for purpose," can save you a lot of money. And as you no doubt knew but now again realize, those savings go straight to your bottom line. It's all part of consolidation before you move on to greater things.

SO NOW JUST DO IT

None of this is world-shocking material. The principles are not that difficult but the sting always lies in the detail, the damned detail. Clausewitz (1780–1831) in his world famous book *On War*, wrote, "Everything in war is very simple, but the simplest thing is incredibly difficult."[2]

The business parallel to this statement is just as valid. The execution of any strategy of taking a business beyond the SENIC phase requires great attention to detail and continuous focus to deal with the many friction points as and when they occur.

And what must become of entrepreneurs who decided that management was not for them and decided to move over? As owners with managers, they still are the owners of the businesses. Ultimate decision power can and must be exercised either individually or through the newly appointed board. If the entrepreneurs fulfilled the role of the creative force for the business, this surely can (and perhaps must) continue in some shape or form. If they did not, then they can either enjoy their hobbies or rent a garage somewhere and start another venture. The economy depends on it!

NOTES

    1. McKinsey as quoted in James O'Shea and Charles Madigan, *Dangerous Company: Consulting Powerhouses and the Companies They Save and Ruin* (London: Nicholas Brealey Publishing Ltd., 1999).

    2. von Clausewitz, Carl, *Vom Kriege* (Berlin: Dümmlers Verlag, 1832), www.clausewitz.com/CWZHOME/Quotations.html, 90–123.

Appendices

APPENDIX A: THE EARLY PART OF A COMPANY'S LIFE CYCLE

Greiner (1972) described the life cycle of companies as a series of evolutionary and revolutionary phases.[1] Each evolutionary or development phase had to be followed by a period of revolution or unrest. The periods of unrest were purported to be an inevitable consequence of the previous development phase. Periods of development were characterized by a dominant management style, while revolutionary periods were characterized by the dominant management problem that had to be solved. The speed at which an organization would experience periods of development followed by interludes of unrest was linked to market conditions and industry sector.

Greiner identified five specific phases of evolution and revolution, which he termed:

Phase 1—Creativity
Phase 2—Direction
Phase 3—Delegation
Phase 4—Coordination
Phase 5—Collaboration

He also made the point that each phase is both an effect of the previous phase and a cause for the next.

The life cycle of any business starts with the innovative or entrepreneurial phase. All efforts are geared towards getting the venture off the ground; there is no time for the niceties of formal systems and procedures. As a consequence this phase is characterized by creation and informality, but also very markedly by the management style of the entrepreneur(s).

As, in general, an entrepreneurial style of management would not be congenial to the development of a business beyond its start-up phase, this management style leads to the first period of upheaval. Thus the predominant management style, entrepreneurial during the first development phase, is the cause of the first period of unrest, namely, the first organizational crisis. The management problem that needs to be solved during this crisis is one of direction and control. A functional organization structure must be developed, authorities and responsibilities are to be allocated, and formal systems ought to be introduced.

The first organizational crisis is the main topic of this book. Businesses that find themselves in this turbulent phase of change are referred to as SENIC—Still Evolving, Now in Crisis—in the main text.

If the first organizational crisis is overcome, a period of evolution, referred to as, direction, is entered that will in time lead to a period of revolution during which the directional style of management is faced by the revolution of delegation.

APPENDIX B: SOME GUIDELINES FOR EMPLOYING CONSULTANTS

Before you employ a consultant, consider whether you can execute the project with your own people or with the help of a contract employee that you can hire in for a specific period.

If you still think the consultant route is the one to take, make sure that:

1. *The project is not "open ended."* Define the assignment as clearly as possible and agree on the time span and the fees. Remember, it's their mission to stay with you as long as possible and optimize their fees. Your mission should be to get them out of the organization as soon as possible.
2. *Make sure you get the services of the senior partner who sold you on the project.* Some consulting companies have the senior people sell the contracts, and then hand them over to junior people to conduct. Don't let that happen to you. Make sure you check the credentials and the reputation of the consultants who are actually going to do the work. There is nothing wrong with inexperienced consultants, but why should they learn at your expense?
3. *Don't be overawed by the big well-known names.* They have all had the normal mix of successes and failures (O'Shea and Madigan, 1999). Sometimes, the smaller practices are more fitting to your own SENIC business. But above all, seek out consultants who have real-life experience in the difficulties you are experiencing.
4. *Beware of the jargon.* Consultants love to create an air of superiority by using all the latest buzz words. Also, they specialize in drawing complex and often incomprehensible diagrams. Insist on an understandable, tailor-made approach for your business, and involve your own staff as much as possible.
5. *Beware of "trendy solutions."* Quite a few of the larger consultancy practices have developed a "template" based on a methodology that is often rooted in one of the latest management trends. Just think of reengineering during the nineties. Junior consultants, often recent MBA graduates, can be trained easily to implement this methodology regardless of the circumstances. If you allow this to happen, your problems are generalized and then fitted into their trendy model. Then the

solution is dished up as being ultimately suitable for your business. Never accept this. Insist on a tailor-made approach.

6. *No one has ever developed a strategy through analytical techniques.* Be particularly careful with consultants that rely heavily on analysis. They are probably expert in data manipulation, formalizing the process of planning, extrapolating the current strategy, or copying the strategy of a competitor. *But they are probably not expert in creating a new strategy for your business.* This point is discussed in more detail in Chapter 2, Section "Decide on What You Want" and Chapter 4, Section "Where, What, and Above All HOW."

7. *Be well aware of what is happening.* Trust your own employees. Quite a few consultants have the tendency to, at best, pay scant attention to the "natives," or, at worst, totally ignore their ideas and suggestions.

8. *Your own managers must be in control.* They must bear the ultimate responsibility for anything the consultants suggest, want to implement, or desire to change. If your management doesn't participate actively, the project is dead before it has started. The consultants will leave in time, but your own people will have to use whatever is left behind.

9. *When you are unhappy with anything at all, make it well known and demand satisfaction.* Don't forget you are the customer and you are paying! Remind yourself that in essence there is no difference between your suppliers and your consultants. They both provide services and/or products that must comply with your wishes and requirements.

APPENDIX C: EXAMPLE OF A PRACTICAL CASH-FLOW CONTROL SYSTEM

Tables C.1 and C.2 present the cash-flow forecast for Widgets on Time, Ltd (WOT, Ltd.), an imaginary small engineering company. Table C.1 records the projected income and Table C.2 predicts the overall cash flow of the company. The current month is January; thus, December has been brought up-to-date to reflect the true flow of cash and the bank balance while January and the following months are forecasts.

WOT Ltd. is forecasting income by means of issued order numbers. Naturally, for your business income forecasting must be based on the most convenient and accurate way. For example, by product group, customer groups or individual key customers with second-tier and third-tier customers and the remainder in groups, and so forth. In the example, the actual numbers are the dollar amounts. (In thousands of dollars—don't be an accountant and start recording numbers in dollars and cents. If WOT Ltd. and you, for that matter, get it right to a couple of thousand, you should be really proud of yourselves!) These dollars are projected for income receipt and have to be paid. Naturally, full cognizance of WOT's or your own credit terms and those of suppliers need to be taken. Don't fool yourself. If your credit terms are thirty days but your average client pays you in sixty, plan for the sixty! To get your money earlier is obviously of vital

Table C.1
Widgets on Time Ltd.—Projected Income in $*000

Order No	Dec	Jan	Feb	Mar	Apr	May	Jun
32455	2.0						
32456	9.7	10.2	10.0				
32457	12.4	12.4	23.6				
32458	13.6	10.6	9.5	3.6			
32459	14.7	14.3	7.8	1.2			
32460			17.4	34.6			
32461	24.6						
32462	6.5	12.7	12.7	12.7	12.7		
32463	14.2						
32464	13.3						
32465		12.4					
32466			17.6				
32467				35.7			
32468					45.8		
32469		12.2	14.7	15.6	16.5	17.2	
32470			9.5	9.5	9.5	9.5	9.5
32471	9.3	9.3	9.3	9.3			
32472	8.4		8.4		8.4		8.4
32473				10.6		12.6	
32474							
32475							
32476							
32477							
32478							
32479							
32480							
32481							
32482							
32483							
32484							
32485							
32486							
32487							
Total Projected Income	126.7	94.1	140.5	132.8	92.9	39.3	17.9

importance, but that requires a debtor strategy and should not affect your cash-flow planning. The cash-flow planning needs to be as realistic as possible under the present conditions. Similar logic applies to your supplier payments. If their terms are ten days but you have gotten away with thirty for some considerable time without them even blinking, plan for the thirty.

Looking at the projected income pattern, it appears that WOT Ltd. is a project organization that has no "steady" income flow. Its projects appear

Table C.2
Widgets on Time Ltd.—Cash Flow Forecast in $*000

	Dec	Jan	Feb	Mar	Apr	May	Jun
Income from Operations	126.7	94.1	140.5	132.8	92.9	39.3	17.9
Sale of Spare Parts	1.9	3.7	2.0	2.0	2.0	2.0	2.0
Sale of Scrap	0.4	0.7	0.5	0.5	0.5	0.5	0.5
Paper Recycling	0.1	0.1	0.1	0.1	0.1	0.1	0.1
Oil Recycling	0.2	0.3	0.3	0.2	0.3	0.2	0.3
Other Sales	2.5	0.4					
Sale of Assets		2.9					
Total Income	**131.8**	**102.2**	**143.4**	**135.6**	**95.8**	**42.1**	**20.8**
Wages & Salaries	21.4	21.4	21.4	21.4	21.4	21.4	21.4
Professional Fees	5.0	1.2	2.0	0.5	0.5	0.0	0.0
Loan repayments	12.7	12.7	12.7	12.7	12.7	12.7	12.7
HP & Lease Agreements	23.0	23.0	23.0	23.0	23.0	23.0	23.0
Interest	4.5	4.5	4.5	4.5	4.5	4.5	4.5
VAT	6.0	6.0	7.2	7.5	7.3	6.4	5.9
Other Taxes	0.0	0.0	0.0	0.0	0.0	0.0	23.5
Purchase—Basic Raw Materials	23.7	20.6	19.4	23.5	24.2	24.2	24.2
Purchase—Aux Materials	10.2	9.7	11.4	9.4	9.6	9.6	9.6
Purchase—Technical	4.6	5.0	5.0	5.0	10.0	5.0	5.0
Purchase—Office Equipment	0.9	1.2	0.6	0.7	0.7	0.8	0.8
Purchase—Other	0.2	0.4	0.3	0.3	0.3	0.3	0.3
Transportation 1	15.5	16.4	15.8	16.8	14.7	15.0	15.0
Transportation 2	7.6	7.1	6.9	7.6	7.3	7.3	7.3
Total Expenditures	**135.3**	**129.2**	**130.2**	**132.9**	**136.2**	**130.2**	**153.2**
Net Cash Flow	**−3.5**	**−27.0**	**13.2**	**2.7**	**−40.4**	**−88.1**	**−132.4**
Bank Pos Start	**−157.6**	**−161.1**	**−188.1**	**−174.9**	**−172.2**	**−212.6**	**−300.7**
Bank Pos Ends	**−161.1**	**−188.1**	**−174.9**	**−172.2**	**−212.6**	**−300.7**	**−433.1**
Facility	−200.0	−200.0	−200.0	−200.0	−200.0	−200.0	−200.0

to last about one to four months, and some sales work still has to be done for April and beyond in order to keep going. WOT Ltd.'s expenditure pattern is about $130,000 per month and it would require the same amount of income to break even, from the cash-flow point of view.

As indicated in the main text, cash-flow forecasting is not an exact science, but, as illustrated in this example of WOT Ltd., it does indicate what needs to happen in sales receipts to keep afloat at the current expenditure level. In general, it certainly should give a good indication whether you are actually "getting ahead" or "just coming up for gulps of air" while "in the drink" fully clothed with that feeling that it's getting more difficult to come up as time goes by!

If your business has a more regular income pattern, cash-flow forecasting can take on a more expected pattern—nice for the short term, but nevertheless keep on monitoring. Regular customers can suddenly start showing irregular order patterns too, and your costs might start rising while you cannot afford to pass on increases in costs to your customers.

APPENDIX D: SAMPLE JOB DESCRIPTIONS

Position: Sales Manager

Purpose of the Job
To market the company's products and achieve sales targets as set by the general manager from time to time.

Main Tasks

- To propose and agree on the sales budget in consultation with the general manager and the MD.
- To proactively market and sell all the company's products in accordance with the sales budget and report on a regular basis.
- To liaise with the logistics manager as to the requirements, capacity, and limitations of the various factory units.
- To monitor the activities in the marketplace with regards to the competition, new product opportunities, and the industry in general.
- To provide the "first" input to the master planning schedule (MPS) as to what has to be done, when, and where.
- To keep adequate records of all quotes provided to potential clients.
- To lead, direct, and control all staff in his department.
- To attend monthly management meetings and ad-hoc project meetings as directed by the general manager.

Short-term Objectives

- Maintain the current level of activity in the AA market and develop the BB market in line with the company's plans.
- Constantly monitor price levels and seek margin improvement.
- Evaluate novel product proposals as to the most effective way of marketing such products.
- With the general manager, develop a set of "standard sales and delivery conditions" for the company.

Position: Production Manager

Purpose of the Job
To produce all products, in the three factory units, according to the required quality and specifications and in accordance with the master planning schedule (MPS).

Main Tasks

- To liaise with the Logistics Departments as to the weekly production schedule and possible changes therein to optimize throughput.
- To meet and if possible exceed production targets.
- To control quality of the manufacturing processes and maintain all records associated with quality of the process and the finished product.
- To effectively maintain all plants and equipment under his control and thereby reduce "down time."
- To report production and maintenance performance to the general manager.
- To lead, direct, and control his production and maintenance supervisors, and through them all staff in his department.
- To attend monthly management meetings and ad-hoc project meetings as directed by the general manager.

Short-term Objectives

- Form part of the team that will decide what planning system, lead times, and constraints will be part of the company's philosophy.
- To develop a set of standard operating procedures for all three factory units.
- To seek optimum staffing for the three factory units and maintain a high level of quality awareness in all members of his staff.
- Implement a system of preventive maintenance for all machinery and equipment under his control.
- Set up a cleaning schedule for all areas under his control in support of the preventive maintenance schedule.
- Attend a supervisory/management course and keep up-to-date on technical issues.

Position: Finance & Administration Manager

Purpose of the Job

To control the company's assets and working capital and in addition maintain an effective personnel record system.

Main Tasks

- To maintain a set of accounts in accordance with the requirements of the business and the suggestions of the company's auditors.
- To prepare the yearly budget and report on actual versus budget on a monthly basis.
- To control and execute the company's payroll.
- To control debtor and creditor accounts within the limits set by the general manager.
- To report on the company's financial results on a monthly basis.
- To maintain adequate records for all personnel with regards to personal information, contracts, salary details, training, disciplinary actions, and all other information required by law or the general manager.

- To manage and control the staff of the department.
- To attend monthly management meetings and ad-hoc project meetings as directed by the general manager.

Short-term Objectives

- Lead the team that will decide what company reports are required and how to monitor the business effectively.
- Manage the cash flow of the business and set up a cash flow system to control debtors and creditors on a weekly basis.
- Divide the business into three units and report on their performance in order to determine their contribution.
- To set up a personnel administration system.
- Attend a supervisory/management course and keep up-to-date on technical issues.

APPENDIX E: RECRUITING A GENERAL MANAGER

Most entrepreneurs need a recruitment consultant[2] to hire a suitable general manager. Have a good look at Appendix B, where I provide some guidelines on how to deal with consultants.

Don't just appoint one. Ask around and get as much information about the various consultants and consultancy practices as you can. Size is not important, not to you, the client, anyway. Recruitment is a one-to-one, personal business, and just because "Worldwide Perfect Fit, Inc." has a beautiful brochure, plush offices, and consultants worldwide does not make it suitable for your SENIC business. Look for consultants who are prepared to disagree with you. One of the techniques I have used to discover this is: Make a number of pretty outrageous statements about a relevant topic, then see how the consultant reacts to these and deals with them in his replies. You are not looking for compliance, you are looking for added value.

The other side of the coin is that you must also "open up" to a recruitment consultant and explain the current true state of play. The better consultants know damned well what the first organizational crisis is all about and that strong leadership is required, but they have to determine the fit between you, your business, and possible candidates.

Insist on well-designed advertisements in a number of suitable media, including the Web. There is nothing wrong with consultant databases, but you want to throw the net as wide as possible. Make sure that the consultant describes the job, the organization, and the job requirements to your liking, but do not exaggerate too much. Let the consultant be the first filter of received applications but be prepared to look at quite a few resumes.

Two contentious items that I must still touch on are industry knowledge and years experience. For the former there are various schools of thought, from "the candidate must have it" to "the candidate does not need it" and all the variations in between. For what it's worth, here is my opinion:

Industry knowledge at general management level is much overrated and is one of the reasons why so many organizations are mediocre and liable to fail. Outside industry experience can be very useful to challenge "the accepted" and consider "the unusual." Most SENIC businesses have a core of very knowledgeable people who know their own process and the industry well. It's the task of general management to channel this knowledge in such a way that an organization runs smoothly and is larger than its individual parts. Undue emphasis for a general manager on functional expertise, for example selling or production skills, invariably means that an entrepreneur is really looking for a "salesperson with an accounting bias," or a "production manager who can also guide the sales force." A general manager is defined[3] as "the manager held responsible for the end results, financial and otherwise, of the SENIC business." That's the one you are looking for if you are serious about recruiting a general manager!

There are no guidelines for years of experience either, but remember: Fifteen years spent in a large competitor organization might be a sign of "stuck in a rut," while fifteen years and fifteen jobs might be a sign of superficiality.

Fortunately, there are no rules. It depends on your preferences and your thoughts for the future. But at this stage, your first filter, look for relevant but also varied experiences, and, above all, clarity. Has the candidate stated what she is looking for and is the resume well laid out? Note that for a candidate, the resume is a single shot at getting a first interview. So if her personal marketing stinks, forget it.

So the filters have been applied, a large number of candidates have disappeared in a basket called "not suitable," and the recruitment consultant has interviewed the short-listed survivors. Insist on reading all the resumes of the short-listed candidates yourself and order them according to your own suitability rating. Ask the recruitment consultant to do the same. This is an ideal opportunity to see whether the recruitment consultant can argue his corner and is not too easily swayed by your arguments. If in doubt, include the candidate into the next round. It's only a two-hour commitment on your part and the recruitment consultant is well paid for his services.

So the day has arrived and you, the owner-manager, will at last be confronted with real-life candidates. The interviews must be held at the company premises.[4] It goes without saying that you have prepared well for this day. You have a list of topics to discuss and questions that you wish to ask. You have agreed upon the script with the recruitment consultant and are prepared to evaluate, as impartially as possible, candidates on your own list of important characteristics. Presentation and first impressions do count, but remember to view each interview afresh. Don't have more than three or four interviews a day. Once more, grade the candidates after the interviews and ask the recruitment consultant to do the same. Differences can be discussed in order to arrive at a second short list, which should be made up of no more than three candidates.

Preparation for the second run is naturally just as important. But you, the entrepreneur, knew that already! You have compiled specific topics that need to be discussed in order to get a more in-depth feeling for each candidate and have discussed this list with the recruitment consultant who has given you his input as well. If a tour of the facilities is appropriate, this is the group you want to do it with. Don't delegate this tour to a subordinate. Away from the formal setting of an interview, quite a few candidates will loosen up a lot. It gives you the opportunity to judge and evaluate and allows them the opportunity to get a feel for the place.

Now I know I probably don't have to say this, but please let the prospective general manager talk. Practice the art of silence. It's amazing what people start to talk about when you are silent or just simply acknowledge what has been asked for. Somehow in these initial informal "tour of the premises" situations, people hate silence and will ask another question or talk away much better. This is really the part of the interview where you have the best chance of observing a candidate who has dropped his guard a bit. Ask any good salespeople—they value the power of their own silence and make good use of it to let a customer convince himself!

After this second round of interviews, a preferred candidate should emerge. A last meeting should take place between yourself and the preferred candidate to discuss remuneration, terms, and conditions. Naturally, you will have discussed this separately with the consultant who should have a good idea what the market value of general managers for a particular size company should be. Pitch the offer at the level you are comfortable with, and prepare a written offer. Give the candidate a few days to think about it and await his decision. Make yourself available for answering questions over the phone during this "gestation" period.

There is always a chance that the preferred candidate wants to negotiate a better deal. Give nothing! Assuming that your original offer was pitched at a reasonable level, you can amend a detail, like telephone costs or moving expenses, but hold on to your basic offer. The major concession that can be made is that after six months you will get together with her, discuss progress, and review the salary details. The latter is a good compromise and allows you to see whether the candidate really fits in. Any prospective general manager eager to prove she can rise to the challenge will see the logic in this.

In the event that your number one candidate declines, the chances are that a number two or three are just as capable. But remember, don't compromise on the areas that are important to you. If your number two and three are not really that suitable, you will have to start again.

To end on a light note, I will give you, the entrepreneur, some examples of real-life mistakes you would never allow yourself to make:

- An entrepreneur that was "too busy." All internal interviews were conducted by his trusted financial controller who, by the way, would have to report to the successful candidate. (Ultimate abdication.)

- Another entrepreneur who said to me, at the last hurdle, "That's my offer and if you don't like it, I have others." (Ultimate flexibility.)
- And an entrepreneur that at the last-round interview said to me, "All that I really want is a good sales manager." (Ultimate short circuit.)

NOTES

1. Greiner, L. E., "Evolution and Revolution as Organizations Grow." *Harvard Business Review* (July–August 1972): 37–46.

2. For the purposes of this book, no distinction is made between headhunters, executive recruiters, management recruiters, recruitment consultants, and so forth. Quite a few of them don't really know the difference anyway and most of them are pretty flexible to your demands. Remember, you're in charge. You're the paying client.

3. Now I know there is a lot of "title" confusion due to inflationary creep. Nowadays (2007) there are functions such as, general manager-accounting, managing director-sales, not to speak of all the C's—titles like, Chief Financial Officer, Chief Purchasing Officer, and similar grandiose sounding ones that have been "invented" to attract the right candidates. Don't be fooled. It's the job that's important. The title is just padding.

4. It is important for candidates to realize where they might be going to work. Don't forget recruitment is a two-way stream and any job candidate must like working for you as much as you want him to work for you.

Bibliography

Berglas, S. "Liar, Liar, Pants on Fire." *Inc. Magazine*, August 1, 1997. www.inc. com/magazine/19970801/1295.html: 1.

Buchanan, L. "The New Face of Confidence." *Inc. Magazine*, February 1, 2003. www.inc.com/magazine/20030201/25115: 1–8.

Collins, J. C., and Moore, D. G. *The Organization Makers: A Behavioral Study of Independent Entrepreneurs*. New York: Appleton-Century-Crofts, 1970.

Collins, J. C., and Porras, J. I. *Built to Last: Successful Habits of Visionary Companies*. New York: Harper Business, 1994.

Drucker, P. F. *Management, Tasks, Responsibilities, Practices*. New York: Harper-Collins, 1985.

Filley, A. C. *Interpersonal Conflict Resolution*. Madison: University of Wisconsin, 1975.

Fingleton, E. *In Praise of Hard Industries: Why Manufacturing, Not the New Economy, Is the Key to Future Prosperity*. London: Orion Publishing Group Ltd., 1999.

Greiner, L. E. "Evolution and Revolution as Organizations Grow." *Harvard Business Review*, July–August 1972: 37–46.

Hamel, G. "Killer Strategies." *Fortune Magazine*, 35, June 23, 1997: 70.

Heiman, S. E., and Sanchez, D. *The New Strategic Selling: The Unique Sales System Proven Successful by the World's Best Companies*. Boston: Warner Books Inc, Rev. ed., 1998.

Hill, L. A. *Becoming a Manager: Mastery of a New Identity*. Boston: Harvard Business School Press, 1956.

Janis, I. L., and Mann, L. *Decision Making: A Psychological Analysis of Conflict, Choice, and Commitment*. New York: Free Press, 1977.

Kennedy, G. *Everything Is Negotiable*. London: Century Business, an Imprint of Random House UK Ltd., 1982.

Mintzberg, H. *Managers Not MBAs: A Hard Look at the Soft Practice of Managing and Management Development*. San Francisco: Berrett-Koehler Publishers, 2004.

Mintzberg, H., Ahlstrand, B., and Lampel, J. *Strategy Safari: The Complete Guide through the Wilds of Strategic Management*. New York: The Free Press, a Division of Simon & Schuster, 1998.

Mintzberg, H., and Waters, J. A. "Tracking Strategy in an Entrepreneurial Firm." *Academy of Management Journal*, 25, No. 3, 1982.

Mintzberg, H. *The Rise and Fall of Strategic Planning*. London: Prentice Hall Europe, 1994.

O'Shea, J., and Madigan, C. *Dangerous Company: The Consulting Powerhouses and the Businesses They Save and Ruin*. London: Nicholas Brealey Publishing Ltd. (updated paperback edition), 1999.

Peter, L. J., and Hull, R. *The Peter Principle*. London: Souvenir Press Limited, 1969.

Peters, T. *Thriving on Chaos: Handbook for a Management Revolution*. New York: Harper Paperbacks, 1988.

Ranft, A. L., and O'Neill, H. M. "The Perils of Power." *MIT Sloan Management Review*, 43, Spring 2002: 13.

Smith, T. *Accounting for Growth: Stripping the Camouflage from Company Accounts*. London: Century Business, an Imprint of Random House UK Ltd., 1992.

Special Report. "Family Business: Passing on the Crown." *The Economist*, November 4, 2004: 2, 5.

Special Report. "The World's Oldest Companies: The Business of Survival." *The Economist*, December 18, 2004: 3.

Welsh, J. A., and White, A. W. "A Small Business Is Not a Little Big Business." *Harvard Business Review*, July 1, 1981: 18–32.

Index

About the Author

THEO J. VAN DIJK is an interim general manager of post-entrepreneurial, growing businesses. He is a specialist in corporate turnarounds and corporate growth and expansion. A Dutch national living in England and Ireland, he works throughout the Western world.